Creating Wire AND Beaded Jewelry

Creating Wire AND Beaded Jewelry

Over 35 beautiful projects using wire and beads

LINDA JONES

NORTH LIGHT BOOKS

Cincinnati, Ohio
www.artistsnetwork.com

Dedication

This book is dedicated to my wonderful boys, Ben and Charlie,
and to all my family, especially my parents.

Distributed to the trade and art markets in North America by
North Light Books
an imprint of F+W Publications, Inc.
4700 East Galbraith Road
Cincinnati, OH 45236
(800) 289-0963

ISBN 1-58180-632-9

First published in the United Kingdom in 2004 by Cico Books Ltd
32 Great Sutton Street London EC1V 0NB

Copyright © Cico Books Ltd 2004
Project designs © Linda Jones 2004
Photography copyright © Cico Books Ltd 2004

Edited by Gillian Haslam
Photography by Jacqui Hurst
Designed by Christine Wood

Printed and bound in China

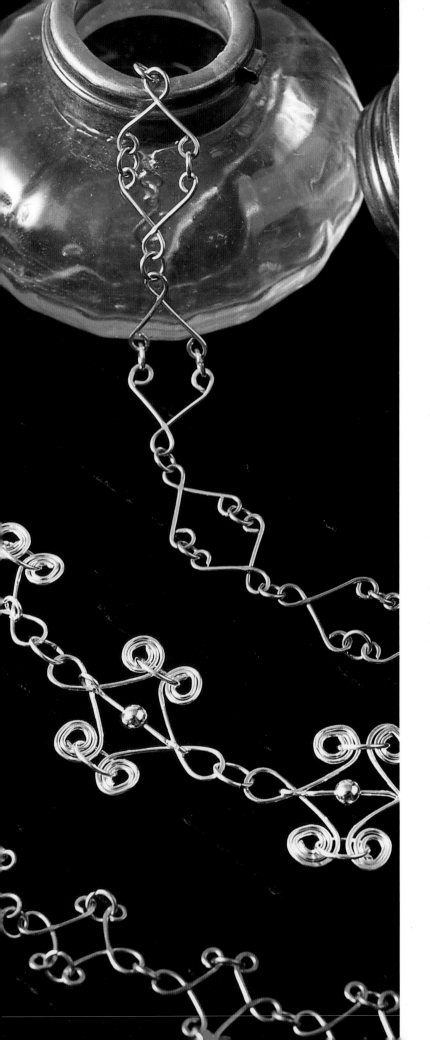

Contents

Introduction

Jewelry is an enriching object. It adorns and embellishes, and has the power to transform everyday outfits into something special.

Wire provides the perfect medium for making your own jewelry. It can be coiled, twisted, formed, bent, and linked together as decorative pieces, without any need for soldering. Designing in this way becomes an original expression of the maker and offers you great freedom and unlimited possibilities.

When designing a piece, you may start by sketching your shapes on paper or making rough, model prototypes out of electrical, fuse, or garden wire. It is important to realize that good designs typically evolve through a number of stages. If you begin with a basic idea or concept, it will usually take a minimum of two or three sketches to develop. Even when you think the piece is completed, it may be necessary to modify or develop it further. Much of your design will be a matter of personal taste, but do give some thought to the key factors outlined in this section.

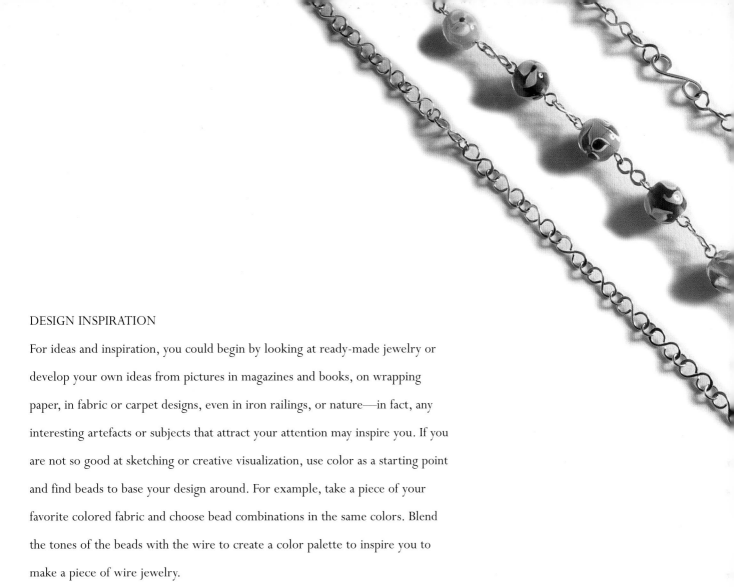

DESIGN INSPIRATION

For ideas and inspiration, you could begin by looking at ready-made jewelry or develop your own ideas from pictures in magazines and books, on wrapping paper, in fabric or carpet designs, even in iron railings, or nature—in fact, any interesting artefacts or subjects that attract your attention may inspire you. If you are not so good at sketching or creative visualization, use color as a starting point and find beads to base your design around. For example, take a piece of your favorite colored fabric and choose bead combinations in the same colors. Blend the tones of the beads with the wire to create a color palette to inspire you to make a piece of wire jewelry.

STYLE

This can also provide you with a starting point for a design. Choose a favorite personal style, such as Art Nouveau, or Egyptian or Celtic art, and so on, and from this foundation you can be inspired by photographs and drawings in books. Extract an element or essence of the style you like as the basis for an idea.

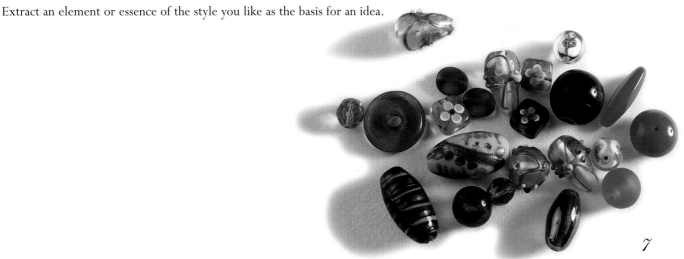

SHAPE AND FORM

Shape and form, size and proportion are all essential elements to making a successful design. Having chosen your style, overall shape and form provide balance and, through symmetry and repetition of shape and/or color, your piece will become esthetically pleasing to the eye.

Modern, abstract shapes can also look extremely striking, but as with any other jewelry design, they must be balanced by proportion. For example, when designing a necklace, the weight of largest shape in the piece should always be at the lowest point.

FUNCTION

As jewelry is not only decorative but has to be worn, you will have to make some practical decisions about the design. Sharp ends are obviously dangerous, and weight and size are also important considerations. For example, earrings that are too heavy will be cumbersome and uncomfortable, and you will find yourself choosing not to wear them. The fittings and findings are just as important as the actual piece of jewelry, as there is no point designing and spending hours creating a beautiful necklace with a weak fastener that falls apart the first time it's worn.

CONTRAST

To add variety, try contrasting different sizes and shapes against each other. Alternatively, contrast line with form, depth with height, or dark against light colors. Textures can also add contrast; with hammered wire placed against highly polished round wire; beads with surface detail against plain manufactured shapes. These contrasts can all be utilized in the same piece of jewelry to create and enhance visual interest.

COLOR

When you are using a selection of beads in one piece, carefully combine complementary tones and blends of hues. Generally, orange and red colors suggest warmth and heat, whilst blues tend to be cold. Using combinations of these two creates bold, striking effects. Every color has a complement and if complementary colors are used adjacently, they will enhance each other to maximum vividness (you only have to look at abstract Modern Art paintings to see this). For example, red is complementary to green, yellow to violet, and blue to orange. This explains why yellow gold has traditionally been used for mounting and setting amethyst stones.

Just remember that the jewelry you are creating is something that will rest on the body and depend on it for display. It should be decorative but also comfortable to wear, a piece you will treasure for years.

Basic Equipment and Techniques

This chapter introduces you to all the basic tools and techniques you need to create your own wire jewelry. You'll see that there's really very little required in the way of special equipment, and the basic techniques are all quick and easy to master, especially if you take a little time to practice on a few lengths of spare wire before beginning the projects that follow.

Whatever your personal style—whether it's modern and minimalist or traditionally classic—once you have mastered the basic techniques, you will be able to create your own unique jewelry designs.

Basic Equipment

Most craft and hobby shops stock all the basic materials and equipment required for simple wirework. However, if you can't find what you need locally, you will be able to obtain everything from jewelry and bead suppliers via the Internet or through mail order catalogs (see page 125 for addresses).

TOOLS

The good news is you will only need three basic tools to begin making wire jewelry:

Round-nosed pliers
Flat-nosed pliers
Wirecutters

As you become more proficient at jewelry-making, you may want to increase your range of tools. Snipe-nosed pliers (also called needle-nosed pliers) are useful for more delicate

wirework, as the ends are more tapered and narrower than flat-nosed pliers. A hammer is essential for texturing, flattening, spreading, and work-hardening wire, and you will need a perfectly smooth and flat steel block to hammer on.

As you progress with this craft and begin creating your own designs, you might wish to experiment with a coiling gizmo—this is a tool that can make wire beads and sprung coils. A jig for creating repeat patterns is also useful when making decorative linking systems.

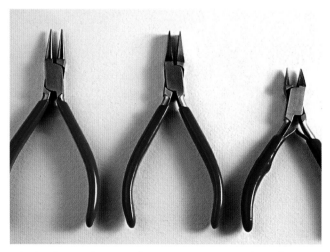

The three basic tools required for creating wire jewelry—from left to right, round-nosed pliers, flat-nosed pliers, and wirecutters.

A small hammer and a smooth steel block with a flat surface—used for flattening and work-hardening wire pieces.

WIRE

Wire is obtainable from most craft and hobby shops and comes in varying gauges and colors. For most basic projects, I recommend that you use 20-gauge (0.8mm) wire, which isn't too flimsy and fine to create wearable jewelry.

The thinner wires—24-gauge (0.6mm) and 28-gauge (0.4mm)—are suitable for twisting together, binding, and wrapping, while the thicker gauges, such as 18-gauge (1mm) and 14-gauge (1.5mm), require a little more experience as they are harder to manipulate. However, they can look very attractive for chunky, bold designs.

Silver- and gold-plated, as well as brass or copper wire can be purchased in measured spools and are flexible and ready to use. Copper wire found in electrical cable, fuse wire, garden wire, and florist wire are also suitable to practice and experiment with. When you become more experienced and wish to create pieces in precious wires, specialist jewelry suppliers provide sterling silver and precious gold wires by measurement. Precious metal wire is usually ordered by length and the price is dictated by weight.

When you manipulate wire, it naturally "work-hardens." This means that you change its structure when you straighten, curl, and form it into your desired shapes. It is important to remember that if you are constantly reworking the same piece of wire, it will first become work-hardened and then begin to lose its flexibility. This means it becomes very brittle and liable to snap or break. Gently hammering wire on a steel block will flatten, texture, and harden it, but be careful not to overdo it. Practice and experience will provide you with a feel for your metal wire.

If you are a complete beginner, cut some small pieces of wire and bend and manipulate them, forward and back, to see how much strain the wire can take. It's far better to do this on wire offcuts than to risk breaking a piece of jewelry.

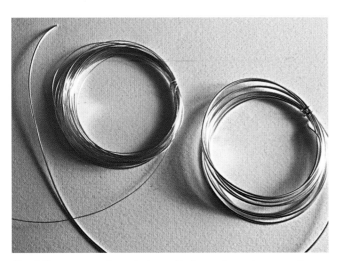

Two different gauges of wire, both suitable for jewelry-making—on the left, 24-gauge (0.6mm) and on the right, 16-gauge (1.2mm).

Three of the most widely available wire colors—copper, silver, and gold. Look in catalogs and on websites for wires in other colors.

Glass beads come in all shapes, sizes, and colors. Some of these have special luster finishes, while others are embellished with painted designs.

BEADS

These can be obtained from craft and specialist jewelry suppliers, or from local charity or thrift shops, boot fairs, trunk and garage sales, and so on. Just tell all your family and friends that you have started making jewelry and I'm sure you'll find that they have old or broken pieces to pass on to you that can easily be taken apart and recycled into something new and original.

Shells, buttons, steel washers, feathers, coins—in fact, anything that looks interesting and attractive can be turned into a design. You can even make your own beads with clay or papier-mâché. You don't have to spend a fortune on beautiful hand-blown glass beads from Venice—as long as you plan your design carefully and balance the colors and sizes of your beads in your piece, you will create beautiful jewelry without having to spend a fortune.

Plastic-lidded boxes divided into compartments provide great storage for your beads, as you can see at a glance what is available.

Seedbeads (also known as rocailles) are some of the smallest beads available. They are excellent for adding small, colorful details.

Metallic beads, whether highly polished or with a matte finish, look great threaded onto wire. They also look good on leather cords.

FINDINGS

These are the ready-made components such as chains, keyrings, hairslides or barrettes, brooch bars, leather cord, clasps, cufflinks, earwires, and so on that can be purchased from craft and hobby suppliers. You will find that it is usually more economical to buy these in small quantities than piece by piece. If you have other friends making jewelry, you could purchase in bulk and split the cost and units between you.

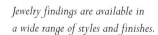

Jewelry findings are available in a wide range of styles and finishes.

Basic Techniques

If you've never attempted making any wire jewelry before, I strongly recommend that you begin by reading this section of the book thoroughly as it explains the basic techniques that are used throughout the step-by-step projects in later chapters. The techniques are all easy to master, and it is well worth practicing them on a few lengths of scrap wire before embarking on your chosen project.

Even though jumprings and clasps can be bought ready-made from suppliers, it is always useful to know how to create them. This will not only add originality to your pieces, but will help to blend all parts together, as a unified piece. For example, a beautiful beaded necklace can be ruined by using a cheap, ready-made clasp that doesn't match the style.

THREADING BEADS WITH WIRE

Once you have perfected this basic principle, you will be able to design and construct necklaces, bracelets, and earrings with all your favorite beads. For your first attempts, begin by practicing with some inexpensive beads (perhaps re-used from an old, broken necklace) and use 20-gauge (0.8mm) copper wire. This wire is very flexible so it is great for beginners. Just ensure that the wire does fit through the drilled holes of the beads with ease.

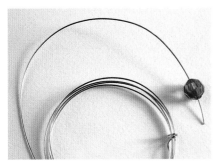

1 Pull the end of the wire out from the coil and thread your chosen bead onto the wire.

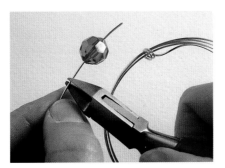

2 Allow just under ⅓in. (1cm) on each side of the bead, and cut this length with the wirecutters.

3 Thread the wire with the bead, then, holding the wire vertically, use the very tips of the round-nosed pliers to bend the wire to a right angle where it touches the bead.

4 Place the pliers about three-quarters of the way up the wire, gripping it tightly, and curl it into a circle, molding it around the circular shaft of the pliers.

5 Turn the bead around and form another link at the other side, in exactly the same way.

6 Practice threading a few beads and then try linking them together. Using flat-nosed pliers, open one of the loops slightly sideways, link it into another, and close and secure it tightly. Ensure all the links are facing in the same direction.

MAKING A HEADPIN

If you want to thread a bead with only one suspension link, you will need to create a headpin at one end. This is done by curling the end of the wire into a tiny hook with the tips of round-nosed pliers. Squeeze this flat and onto itself with flat-nosed pliers, thereby creating a "knob" at one end (this will prevent the bead slipping off). Create a link at the other end by following steps 1 to 4, above.

Creating Spirals

There are two sorts of spirals—the "open" (with space around the spiral) and the "closed" (a tight coil). Begin

by learning how to create a closed spiral with 20-gauge (0.8mm) copper wire, as this will give you the skill

and experience to approach the open spiral, which needs slightly more control and practice.

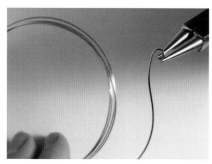

1 You can work directly from your coil of wire, or cut a piece at least 3—4in. (7.5—10cm) in length. Start by forming a very small circle at one end of the wire, using the end of the round-nosed pliers. (Try to ensure this first stage is as circular as possible, as the rest of the spiral will be formed around it.)

2 Grip this circle tightly in the flat-nosed pliers and continue curling the wire around itself in the same direction, increasing its diameter at every turn.

3 When the spiral is large enough, or if you've used up all your wire, curl the projecting cut end into a small loop in the opposite direction to the spiral. The spiral can now be suspended from this link.

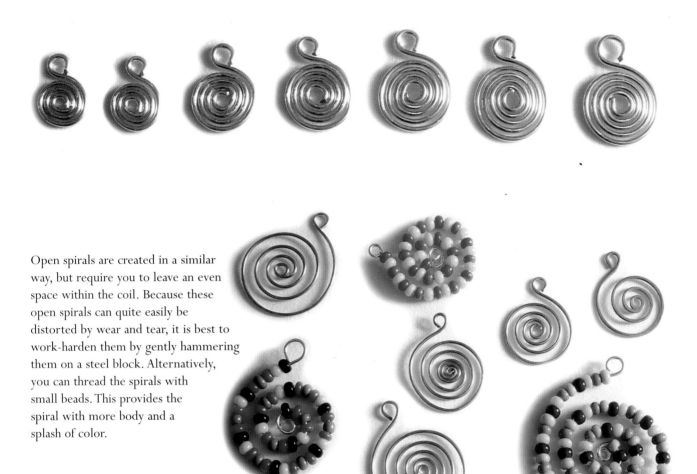

Open spirals are created in a similar way, but require you to leave an even space within the coil. Because these open spirals can quite easily be distorted by wear and tear, it is best to work-harden them by gently hammering them on a steel block. Alternatively, you can thread the spirals with small beads. This provides the spiral with more body and a splash of color.

A further alternative is to create uneven spirals. These are formed in a similar way as the open spirals above, but are made by curling the wire in short, sharp movements with pliers. Hammer the pieces on a steel block to flatten and work-harden them.

This pair of silver earrings was created by making two closed spirals (with flat-pad earring backs glued on behind), with two hammered and uneven spirals linked on as pendants. Both spirals are simple yet attractive designs and go well together.

Making Jumprings

Jumprings are the most elemental links you can create. They can serve as a unit in multiple numbers for a chain, or can be used to join (or jump) a series of other units together, as in a beaded necklace or bracelet.

It is best to make a number of jumprings at the same time. They can be made in a variety of gauges and diameters of wire and kept for future use once constructed. The rings are made in two different ways—see steps 1 and 2, below.

1 The first method is to wrap the wire around the same spot on one of the tapered ends of your round-nosed pliers, thus creating an even, cylindrical spring.

2 Alternatively, take a knitting needle or cylindrical dowel (of the same diameter you wish to make the rings) and wind the wire tightly around it in a coil.

3 When you've created the "spring," find the cut end and snip up through to the next coil above, thereby cutting off a perfect jumpring. Cut the whole spring in this way.

4 As solder is not used in this book, you will need to work-harden or temper each ring as you close it. To link the rings together, always open them sideways with flat-nosed pliers, to avoid distorting the shape, and link into one another, closing the join by gently moving one wire just past the other. This ensures that the wire wants to spring back onto the cut join and close on itself.

Try creating two different jumpring diameters and linking them together, alternating the ring sizes, to make a decorative chain. Experiment with two or more jumprings linked together—this will not only make the piece stronger, but will provide a chunkier appearance. Another option is to thread small beads onto your jumprings before you close them, to add variety and a dash of color.

Making S Links

These decorative links can be joined together with jumprings or interspersed with threaded beads to create attractive chains for bracelets and necklaces. Experiment by combining different colors, gauges, and sizes of "S" link units to obtain a variety of ornamental chains.

As with creating any chain or duplicated linking system, it is very important to work in stages to ensure the individual units retain as much similarity in style and size as possible. For example, it is best to begin your project by cutting all the lengths of wire to the same size, and then curl each length with your round-nosed pliers. Only when each individual unit has been constructed, only then should you connect them together to complete your piece of jewelry.

1 To create each unit, cut 1in. (2.5cm) lengths of 20-gauge (0.8mm) wire.

2 Using round-nosed pliers, curl one end of the wire around the center of the circular shaft, forming a loop.

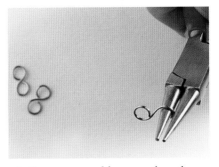

3 Form a second loop on the other side of the wire, curling it in the opposite direction, creating a figure-of-eight shape. (These units can be hammered to work-harden and flatten them.) Link all units together, using jumprings in between, to form a chain. Before you connect each "S" link, ensure that you have closed any gaps with flat-nosed pliers.

Clasps and Fasteners

There are several different styles and types of fastener you can make, so choose one to complement the design of your piece of jewelry, rather than using a ready-made clasp in a different wire bought from a craft shop.

FISH HOOK FASTENER

The fish hook (shown on the far left of the photograph above) is one of the simplest and most versatile jewelry fasteners you can create. It can be made in 20-gauge (0.8mm) wire, or select a thicker gauge of wire if you require something a little chunkier and stronger, to suit your piece of jewelry.

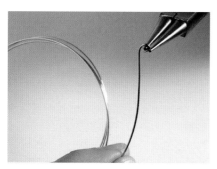

1 Curl the very end of your wire into a very small circle, using just the tips of your round-nosed pliers.

2 Position the pliers on the other side of the wire, just under this first circle and curl around the round-nosed pliers in the opposite direction. Cut the wire, leaving just under ⅓in. (1cm)—enough to create a link.

3 Turn this extended wire into a small loop, ready for linking onto your necklace or bracelet. To provide your clasps with more strength, give them a gentle tap with a hammer on a steel block.

THE EYE OF THE FASTENER

1 To create the circular shape, wrap your wire around the widest part of your round-nosed pliers, or around a cylindrical dowel, approximately 1in. (2.5cm) in from the end.

2 Bind this projecting end around the "stem" wire and secure. Leave just under ½in. (1cm) to make the end loop (with the "stem" wire), which can be used to connect to your necklace or bracelet.

3 To work-harden the unit, place it on your steel block and gently tap the end of the circular loop with your hammer. Take care not to tap the stem where the wire is wrapped around as this would weak it.

4 Using your round-nosed pliers, add the suspension link.

"S" LINK FASTENER

This fastener can look very attractive if your chain or necklace has wire "S" link units incorporated into it, providing your necklace or bracelet with a sense of seamless continuity. For practice purposes, use 20-gauge (0.8mm) copper wire before using silver or gold wire for an actual piece of jewelry.

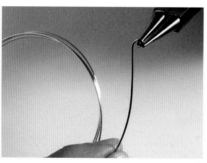

1 Begin by cutting a 2in. (5cm) length of wire. Curl a tiny loop at one end with the tips of your round-nosed pliers.

2 Place the widest part of the pliers on the other side, just under the first loop, and curl the wire around into a larger, curvy shape.

3 Turning the piece around, create the same shape at the other end in mirror image. To work-harden or strengthen the wire, gently hammer it on a steel block.

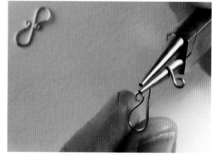

4 Close one of the hooks when you attach it to your finished piece, so that there is only one opening. This decorative unit can also be used as a multiple linking system in chainmaking.

EXTRA-STRONG HOOK

As a double thickness of wire is used here, this fastener is ideal to attach to a bracelet as it is much sturdier than the simple fish hook fastener. Practice making this first in 20-gauge (0.8mm) copper wire.

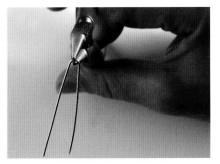

1 You will need to cut at least 3in. (7.5cm) of 20-gauge (0.8mm) wire. Using the tips of your round-nosed pliers, fold the wire in two.

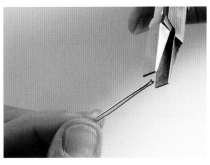

2 With your flat-nosed pliers, squeeze the wires together so that they run parallel.

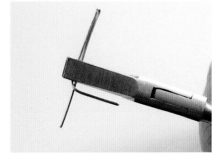

3 Leaving about 1in. (2.5cm) of doubled wire, use flat-nosed pliers to bend the end of one wire, so that the two wires are at right angles to one another.

4 Wrap this turned out wire around the main stem of wire to secure. Snip off any excess wire.

5 Place your round-nosed pliers at their widest point about three-quarters of the way up the doubled wire, and curl the doubled wire down, shaping it around the circular shaft of the pliers to form a hook.

6 Curl the tip of your hook up into a small lip, using the tips of your round-nosed pliers.

7 Finish off the other end of the fastener by using round-nosed pliers to create a small loop to attach and link to your necklace or bracelet.

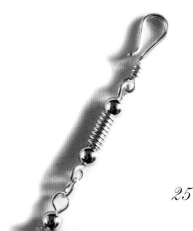

T-BAR CLASP

You can purchase some very attractive, ready-made bar-and-ring clasps from craft and jewelry suppliers. However, if you want to create your own to blend with the wire used in your handmade necklace or bracelet, try this T-bar clasp.

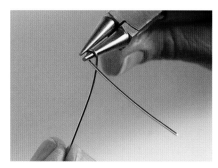

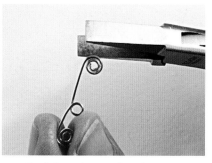

1 Cut a 3in. (7.5cm) length of 20-gauge (0.8mm) wire. Find the center with the tips of your round-nosed pliers and fold both ends around, crossing the wires over in opposite directions.

2 Curl one end of the wire into small spirals, by making little loops at each end. Neatly work the wire in a circular motion around itself, keeping it on a level plane in your flat-nosed pliers.

3 Curl the other end in the same way, leaving a small space between the center, as shown.

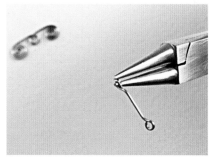

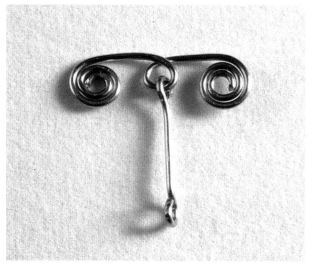

4 Cut another 1in. (2.5cm) piece of wire and curl small loops at each end. Link one end to the center of the T-bar and the other end to your piece of jewelry.

The ring end, or "eye" of the clasp, is created by following steps 1 to 3 of the Eye of the Fastener instructions (see page 23).

Decorative Chainmaking

Making chains by hand is very rewarding so experiment with different linking systems to come up with your own combination. Don't worry too much if the units are not identical as this will not be so evident when the chain is made into one piece. This will also add to its charm and originality. The most important consideration is that all your links are well closed and work-hardened. Spend a little time going over each connection to ensure it is securely fastened and will hold together—you don't want the piece to fall apart when it is worn. As you are going to be making identical, multiple units, work in stages, completing each stage before starting the next. This will help, as you will gain practice by repetition.

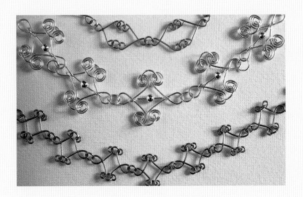

Once you have mastered the chainmaking techniques featured in this chapter, you will be able to create endless variations, as shown with these eyelet chains.

Eyelet Chain

The eyelet chain is a simple yet attractive multiple linking system. Experiment by creating the units in one colored metal, connected by links made in another color. In the photograph below, the eyelet chain is featured on the far right, with the two variations shown beside it (see page 33 for details).

YOU WILL NEED

20 gauge (0.8mm) wire
Round-nosed pliers
Wirecutters
Hammer and steel block

1 To make the basic units, begin by cutting 1½—2in (4—4cm) pieces of 20 gauge (0.8mm) wire. For a standard length bracelet, you will need at least ten units.

2 Find the center of each wire piece with the wider part of your round-nosed pliers and bend it around to form a downward "U" shape.

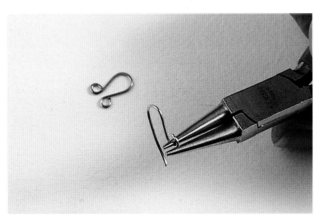

3 Using the very ends of your round-nosed pliers, curl the ends of the wire outward on each "U" piece, to form tiny, closed circles.

4 Shape each piece by placing it back into the widest part of the round-nosed pliers and pinching the sides together around the circular shaft. (If you wish, you can lightly tap each of these units with a hammer on a steel block to flatten and work-harden them.)

5 Connect the units together with jumprings (see page 20). Create a fish hook fastener (see page 22) for the end of the chain.

Spiraled Eyelet

To create this pretty spiraled chain, cut 5in. (12.5cm) lengths of 20-gauge (0.8mm)

wire for each piece. Follow the instructions for the eyelet chain, but in step 3, form

flat spirals with the ends of the wire (see page 18). You will also need larger jumprings

to connect the units together (see page 20).

Eyelet Variation

This chain is created in exactly the same way as eyelet chain on pages 30–32. Follow

all the steps from 1 to 5, but just link your units "back to back" for a contrasting look.

Lattice Chain

The decorative linking system of the lattice chain, featured at the bottom of the photograph below, comprises a multiple "hanger" unit. It is more elaborate than the eyelet chain on page 30, and beads can be suspended from the middle, as shown in the silver variation in the center of the photograph.

YOU WILL NEED

20-gauge (0.8mm) wire
Wirecutters
Round-nosed pliers
Hammer and steel block

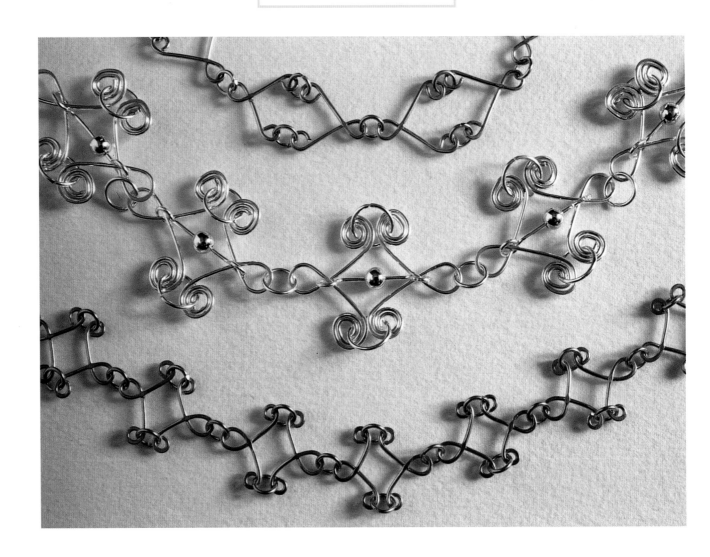

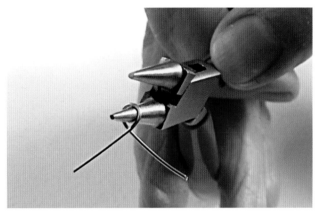

1 To create the lattice shown at the base of the photograph, you will need approximately 1½—2in. (4—5cm) of 20-gauge (0.8mm) wire for each unit. For this standard bracelet 16 units were needed. However, this could vary depending on the unit size you create, or the size of your wrist.

2 Find the center of each piece of wire and, using your round-nosed pliers, neatly cross the wires over in opposite directions.

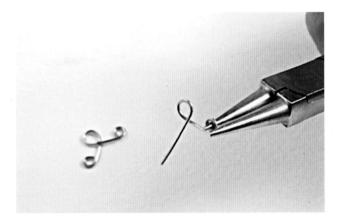

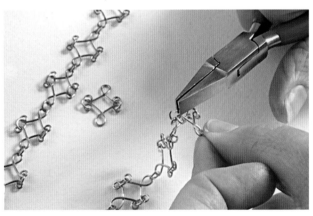

3 Using the very tips of your round-nosed pliers, curl the ends of the wire outward into little circles. (If you wish, you could gently hammer each unit on a steel block to flatten and work-harden. However, be careful not to hammer over the crossed-over wires, as this will only weaken the unit.)

4 Once you have created all your hanger units, position them as shown and link them together using jumprings (see page 20). To complete the chain, make a fish hook clasp (see page 22).

Spiraled Lattice

To create this alternative version of the lattice chain, you will need to cut 5in.

(12.5cm) pieces of 20-gauge (0.8mm) wire for each unit. A wire threaded with

a silver bead was used to connect the center of the units, and larger jumprings

reach through and connect onto the spirals.

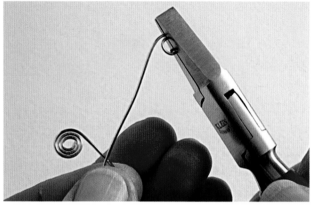

1 To begin making each unit, follow step 2 of the lattice chain, creating a central loop around your round-nosed pliers with each wire crossing over in opposite directions. Spiral these projecting wires (see page 18).

2 Create a number of large jumprings (see page 20). Using flat-nosed pliers, connect these between the spirals, linking the units together.

3 Continue linking all the units together until you have formed your desired length of chain.

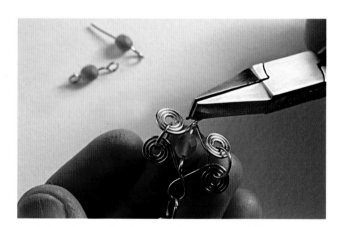

4 Thread some beads onto wire (see page 17) and connect these to the central loops of your units.

Inverted Lattice

To make this attractive inverted lattice chain, follow steps 1 and 2 of the standard

lattice design. However, in step 3, you will need to curl the ends of the wire inward,

instead of outward with the tips of your round-nosed pliers.

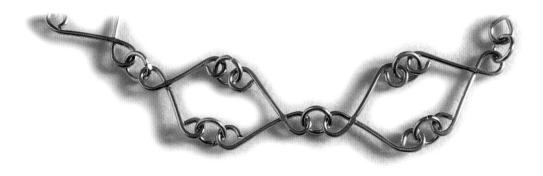

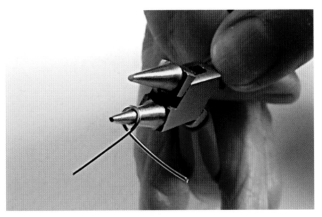

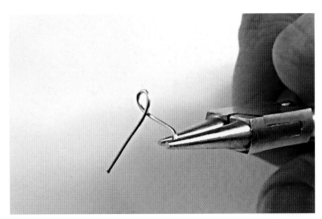

1 Follow steps 1 and 2 of the lattice chain (see page 35), crossing the wires over in opposite directions, using your round-nosed pliers.

2 Curl the ends of the wire inward, to create small loops on either side. Create jumprings (see page 20) and link all the units together to create the chain shown above. Add a fastener of your choice (see pages 22—26) to complete the necklace.

Wiggly Wire Chain

As each unit of this chain is unique, you can work directly from the wire coil. It's just a question of wiggling the wire, first one way and then the other, around the shaft of your round-nosed pliers. With a little bit of practice you will get into a rhythm and the units should take on a pleasing similarity.

YOU WILL NEED

20-gauge (0.8mm) wire
Wirecutters
Round-nosed pliers
Hammer and steel block

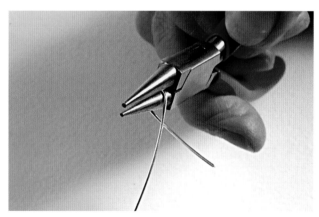

1 Begin by making the end fastener of your bracelet. Form the wire around your round-nosed pliers, creating a loop.

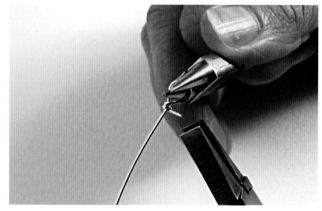

2 Next, wrap the extended length of wire around itself to secure the loop (you may need to use an extra pair of pliers to help hold the wire).

3 Bend the wire around your round-nosed pliers to create the wiggly shapes. Cut the wire off the coil, leaving a 1in. (2.5cm) end. Finish off by creating a link at the end of the wire.

4 To make the other units, form a top link using your round-nosed pliers and continue forming the wire into a wiggly shape so it blends with all the other units. Make as many units as you require.

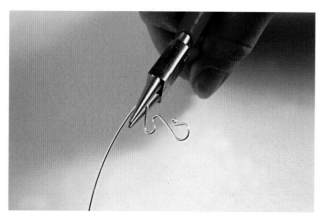

5 To create the end fastener of your chain, curl a fish hook (see page 22) into the wire and continue forming a wiggly shape.

6 Spend a little time compressing each unit together, so that there are no gaps between the wiggles. Gently hammer them on a steel block to flatten and work-harden.

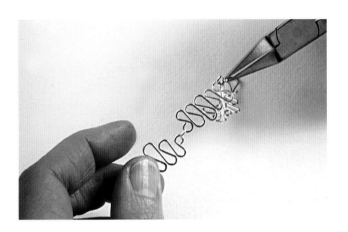

7 Make some jumprings (see page 20) and, using flat-nosed pliers, connect all the units together to form an original and unique chain.

Variations

When you are forming the "wiggles" in your units, you can thread some small beads onto the wire between each bend or alternate bend. You could also thread a bead onto the jumprings to add color and decorative interest. However, do not work-harden your units by hammering, as the beads will shatter.

Create the chain exactly as shown in the steps, but place a colored bead threaded with wire in between each wiggly unit. This can look very attractive on a necklace.

Rings, Brooches, and Bangles

As well as necklaces, bracelets, and earrings, wire can be formed into other accessories. In this section, we show you how to create a strikingly simple ring, a beautiful coat or dress brooch, and an attractive bead bangle. The basic principles of each of the projects will provide you with enough information to experiment and evolve further designs, using your own choice of beads and different gauges and colors of wire.

Beads and wire make the perfect partners, as demonstrated by this dazzling, easy-to-make collection of colorful, glitzy rings, cheerful beaded bangles, and stylish spray brooches.

Bead Spray Brooch

This delicate brooch looks very attractive pinned to a jacket lapel, or worn on a smart, single-color sweater or dress. You can choose any colored beads that blend together or create something that is quite classic, perhaps using a traditional combination of pearl beads with gold wire.

YOU WILL NEED

28-gauge (0.4mm) wire
20-gauge (0.8mm) wire
Beads
Masking tape
Superglue (optional)
Wirecutters
Round-nosed pliers
Ready-made brooch fitting

1 Cut 4—5in. (10—12.5cm) lengths of 28-gauge (0.4mm) wire. Thread each bead or combination of beads onto the center of the wires, then fold the wires down on each side of the bead or beads.

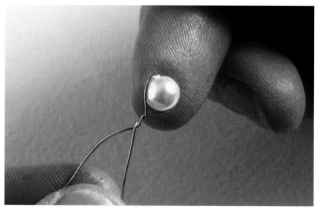

2 Bring both wires together around the bead and twist, securing the bead at the end.

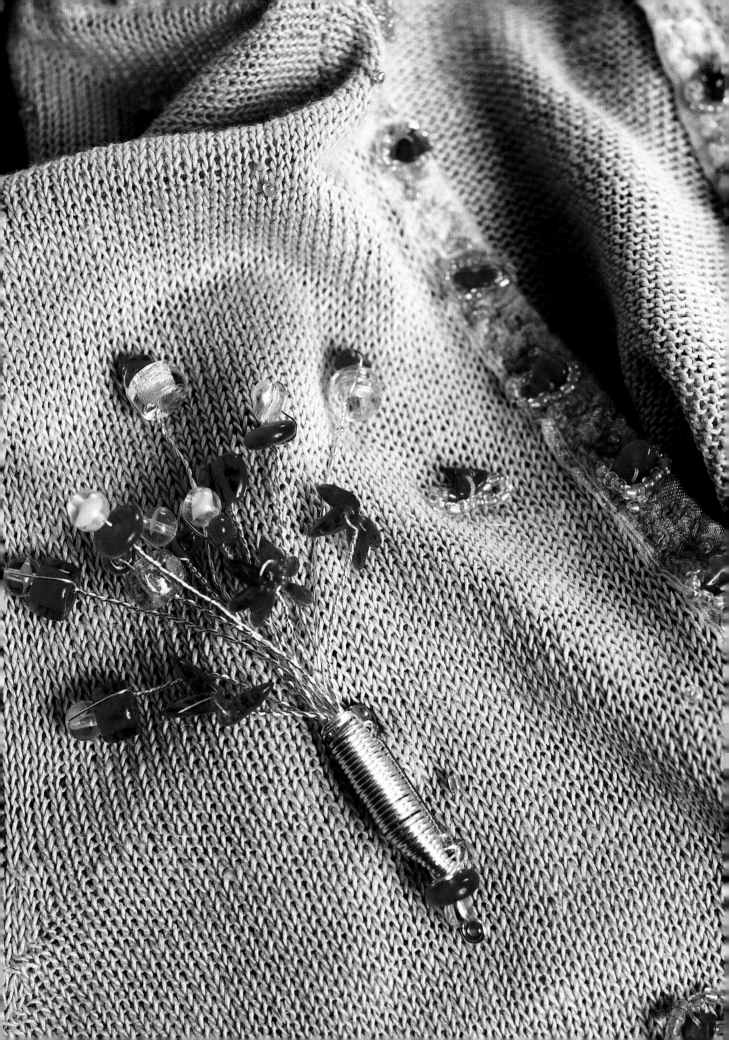

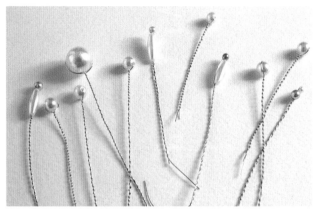

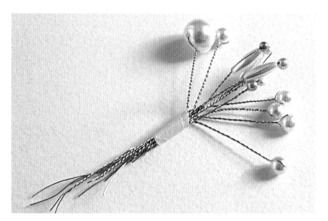

3 Continue twisting all the beads (about eight to ten strands) onto the 28-gauge (0.4mm) wire in this way until you have a pleasing combination or bouquet.

4 Place the wire stems together in a bunch with the heads at an even height, then bind the stems together with masking tape to secure them in position.

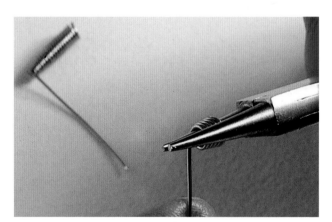

5 Using 20-gauge (0.8mm) wire, form a tube or coil by binding the wire around the shaft of your round-nosed pliers or a cylindrical object. Leave at least 1in. (2.5cm) of wire extending from the coil.

6 Place the stems of your bead bouquet into this coiled tube, hiding the masking tape, and secure around the bunched wires, by squeezing the top rung of the coil tightly around the stems.

7 Thread an extra bead onto the extended wire of the
coil and turn the end into a spiral, to prevent the bead
sliding off. (If you wish, dab a little superglue around the
20-gauge (0.8mm) coil, to ensure the stems of the wired
beads are firmly secured within the tube.)

8 Using 28-gauge (0.4mm) wire directly from the spool,
bind the brooch finding securely to the back of the
bouquet stems.

9 Spend a little time gently adjusting
the angles of the sprays of beads
so that they form an attractive
arrangement. To avoid the brooch
catching on other clothing, it is best
to keep the arrangement fairly flat,
so that it lies close to your body.

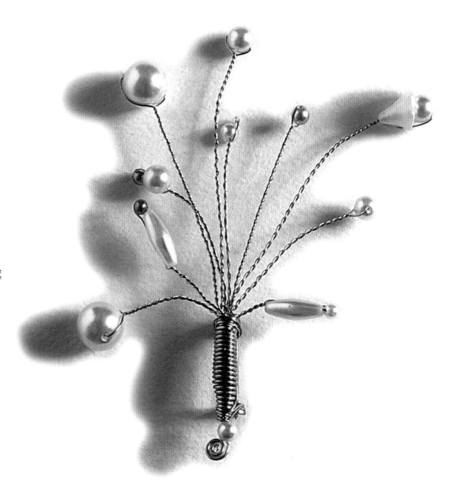

Simple Bead Ring

Although this is such a simple ring to construct, it does look very

impressive purely on account of the beautiful, colored bead. The

cylindrical dowel used to shape the wire in step 1 needs to be slightly smaller

than the size of your finger as the wire will spring open and expand slightly.

YOU WILL NEED

20-gauge (0.8mm) wire
28-gauge (0.4mm) wire
for binding
A cylindrical dowel
A "feature" bead
Wirecutters
Round-nosed pliers

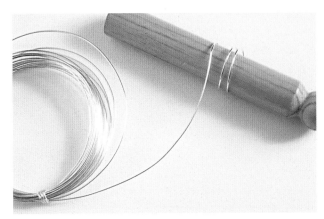

1 Pull out some wire from a 20-gauge (0.8mm) spool and wrap this twice around the cylindrical dowel. Cut the wire just past the point where it overlaps itself.

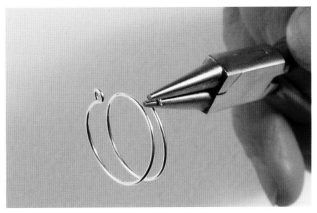

2 Using the tips of your round-nosed pliers, curl the ends of the wire back on themselves to form two small, neat loops.

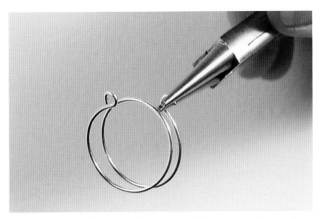

3 Turn these loops 90 degrees, so they sit at right angles to the rest of the ring shank. (If the shank distorts slightly at any stage, simply place it back on the cylindrical dowel and re-shape.)

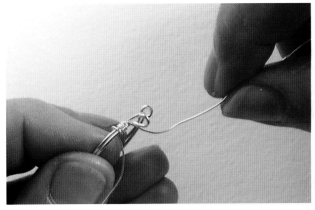

4 Using fine 28-gauge (0.4mm) wire, begin evenly binding the round shank ¼in. (6mm) away from the center of the ring. Do not cut the wire when you have finished binding.

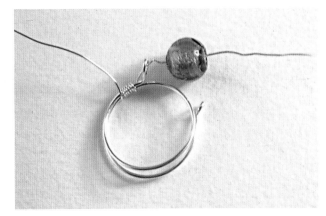

5 Thread the fine wire through one of the loops created in step 2, then thread the wire through the hole in your chosen bead.

6 Continue threading the fine wire through the second loop and finish off by binding around the shank on the other side. If you wish, you can bind the entire shank.

Beaded Bangle

This collection of bangles is colorful and fun, and will instantly brighten up any outfit. You could use a variety of differently colored and shaped beads together, or build up a repeat pattern, as shown here. Wear them on their own or sport several together, in a mixture of colors and styles. And for something a touch more exotic, try suspending some pendant charms intermittently between the beads using jumprings.

YOU WILL NEED

20-gauge (0.8mm) wire

Good selection of beads

Round-nosed pliers

Flat-nosed pliers

Wirecutters

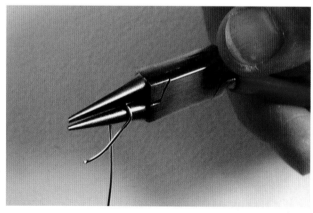

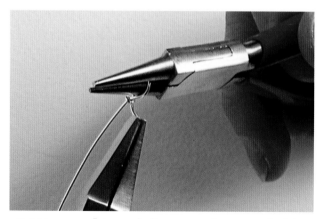

1 To find out how much wire you will require to make the bangle, measure your wrist (a piece of string or cord will do for this) and add approximately 4in. (10cm) to this length. Place your round-nosed pliers about 1in. (2.5cm) from the end of the wire and form a loop by wrapping it around one of the circular shafts.

2 Using your flat-nosed pliers, wrap the very end of the wire around itself and cut off any excess.

3 Thread your chosen beads onto the wire in the desired sequence until you are left with a length of wire measuring approximately 1½—2in. (4—5cm). This will be sufficient for your clasp. (Here the colored beads have been separated by tiny silver beads, creating a small space between the brighter colors.)

4 To create the clasp, using round-nosed pliers, fold the remaining wire so it is doubled, leaving just enough single thickness wire to wrap around the bracelet, close to the last bead.

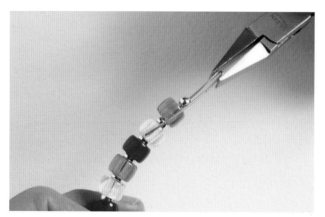

5 Gently squeeze the ends of the two wires together using your flat-nosed pliers.

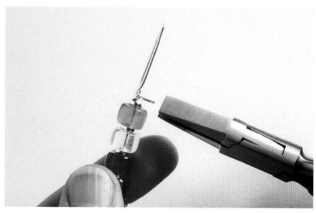

6 Using flat-nosed pliers, carefully wind the wire around itself to secure.

7 Fold the wire around your round-nosed pliers, about three-quarters of the way up, to form a hook. Bend the very end of this hook into a small lip with the end of your round-nosed pliers (see page 25, step 6).

8 Shape the bracelet into a circle by pressing it around a cylindrical object that is smaller in diameter than the bracelet—this gives the bracelet a springiness, enabling it to keep its shape.

Metallic Bangle

Instead of threading on only beads, you can also use uncut coils of wire jumprings as spacers between the beads to give a different look to your bracelet. This method is particularly good for making extra-special beads stand out. See the instructions on page 20 for making jumprings.

Wrapped Jewelry

Wire lends itself to being wrapped and coiled because of its wonderful flexibility. In this section, we show you how to create a "cage" for a bead, encase a glass marble to make a stunning pendant, and fashion an attractive wrapped bead necklace and earring set. These projects are particularly successful when used with inexpensive beads, especially plastic ones, as the technique can make the piece appear very exclusive and expensive as the beads are half-hidden behind the wire. Once you have mastered the simple technique, experiment with wrapping stones and shells to suspend as pendants.

When wrapped in spirals of wire, everyday glass marbles are transformed from a child's traditional plaything into a sophisticated piece of jewelry, with no trace of its humble beginnings.

Caged Bead Necklace

These miniature wire cages can be filled with shells, rock chips, crystals, fabric

scraps, ribbon, scented pot-pourri, dried rosebuds, and, of course, beads! The

½in. (1cm) diameter beads used in this project needed approximately 6in. (15cm)

of 20-gauge (0.8mm) wire for each cage.

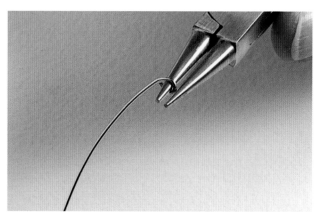

1 The length of the wire required for the cage is dependent on the size of the bead. Using the tips of your round-nosed pliers, begin by creating a small circle at each end of the wire, curling it in opposite directions.

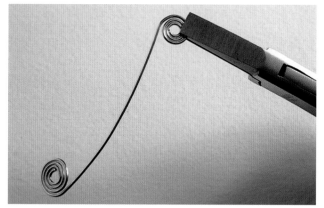

2 Holding one of the small circles within the jaws of your flat-nosed pliers, carefully curl the wire around itself several times to form a neat, flat spiral. Repeat at the other end in the opposite direction.

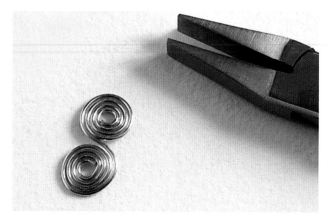

3 Continue coiling the wire into spirals at each end, ensuring they are a similar diameter, until they meet each other in the center (like an "S" shape).

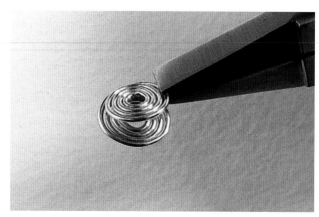

4 When the all the wire has been used and both spirals are formed and touching each other, fold one spiral on top of the other and flatten, using flat-nosed pliers.

5 Carefully pull the central circles out from each spiral at right angles, by placing the round-nosed pliers on the central spiral.

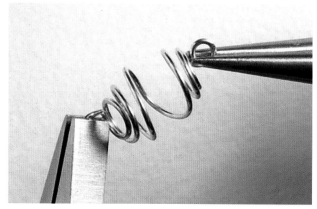

6 Gently pull out these loops, extending the spiral and prizing open the spaces between each coil, using both pairs of pliers. Even out the spaces between the spirals.

7 Using your fingers, prize open the center of the cage carefully and place your selected bead inside the middle of the extended wire spiral.

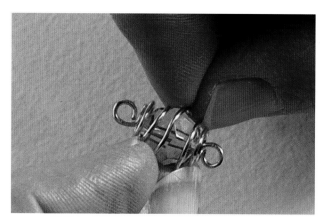

8 Press the wire cage gently around the bead and even out the coils. Use your fingers for this stage as pliers could bend the wire.

9 Link the caged bead onto a chain using jumprings (see page 20). Make as many caged beads as you feel suitable for the design of your necklace.

Caged Bead Earrings

This pretty pair of matching drop earrings is made by first completing steps 1 to 8 of the caged bead necklace,

then by following the two steps shown below to attach the ready-made earwires.

1 Using flat-nosed pliers, fold one of the spiral ends in, next to the encased bead.

2 Make another identical caged bead. Suspend each from a ready-made earwire.

Encasing a Marble

This technique can be used to encase beads, as well as marbles of any size. Just reduce or increase the wire as required. To make a necklace, a chain, black cord, or leather thong is suitable for suspension. Alternatively, the encased marble makes an excellent keyring pendant (see page 62).

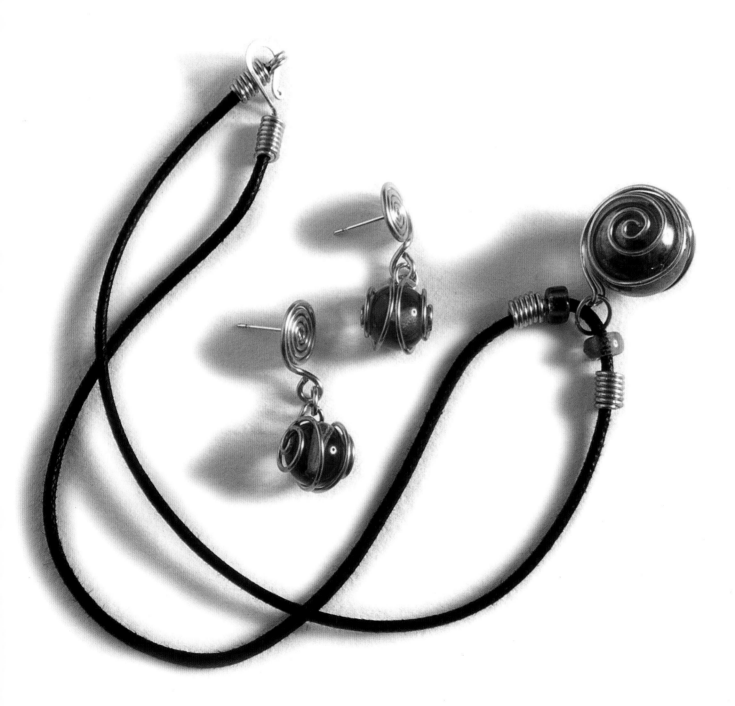

YOU WILL NEED

20-gauge (0.8mm) wire

A standard marble

Round-nosed pliers

Flat-nosed pliers

Wirecutters

1 If you are using a standard small-sized marble, cut approximately 8—9in. (20—23cm) of 20-gauge (0.8mm) wire. Curl each end of the wire into little circles in toward each other, using your round-nosed pliers.

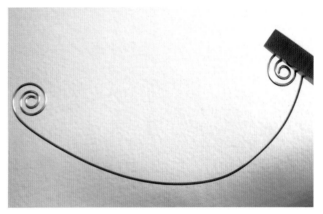

2 Using flat-nosed pliers, create open spirals at each end, curling the wire in, toward each other. Ensure both spirals are of a similar diameter (and stop when the open spirals are the same diameter as the marble).

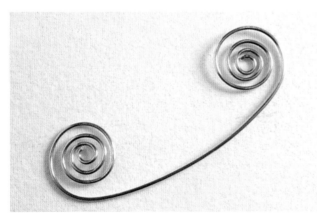

3 Leave a straight, uncurled length of wire measuring approximately 2in. (5cm) between the spirals.

4 Find the center with the tips of your round-nosed pliers and pull the spirals down on each side.

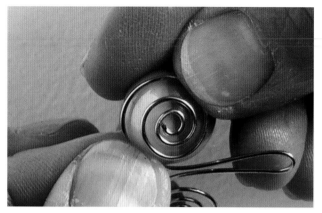

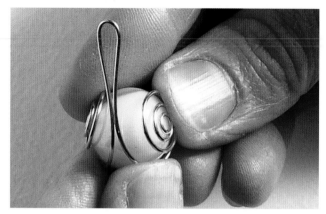

5 Using your fingers so you don't crush the wire, push the marble into one of the spirals.

6 Gently ease the remaining wire spiral around the other side of the marble.

7 Fold the top loop around the marble, pressing it down with a finger. Adjust the spirals and mold them neatly around the marble.

8 Lift the very end of the loop up into a "lip" using the tips of your round-nosed pliers.

9 Add a jumpring to provide a link for a chain (see page 20), a keyring, or whatever suits the design of your piece of jewelry.

Marble Keyrings

These encased marbles are just perfect for attaching to ready-made keyrings (these findings are available from most craft or hobby outlets). You could use differently colored marbles for each member of the household, so everyone can instantly tell which is their own set of keys.

Spiral End Fastener for a Cord or Thong

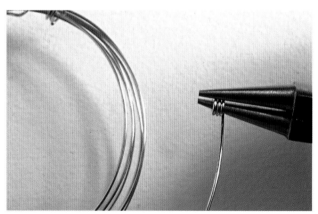

1 If you decide to connect the piece to a leather thong, you can create the end fastener by making two "springs" or coils of wire that fit over the thong diameter (just as you would create jumprings, see page 20).

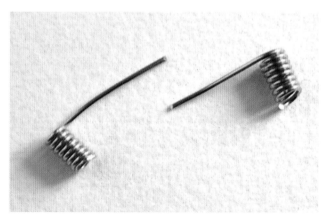

2 Leave 1in. (2.5cm) of straight wire at the ends, then cut off the wire from the spool.

3 Curl the extended wire around your round-nosed pliers to form a circle at right angles to the spiral.

4 Cut the thong to the desired length. Thread the encased marble onto the thong. Now place the cylindrical, coiled sleeves over the ends of the thong and squeeze the last rung of the coil tight against the thong to secure using flat-nosed pliers. (If you wish, add a little dab of clear, strong glue for extra support.)

5 Make a fish hook fastener made from the same type of wire (see page 22) and connect it to one of the right-angled ends, so that you can open and close the back of your necklace.

Wrapped Bead Necklace with Tassel

This stylish design is perfect for using up inexpensive beads and turning them into something

fantastic. Here blue beads are used with silver wire—a classic combination that always works well.

YOU WILL NEED

20-gauge (0.8mm) wire

Beads

Ready-made chain

Round-nosed pliers

Flat-nosed pliers

Wirecutters

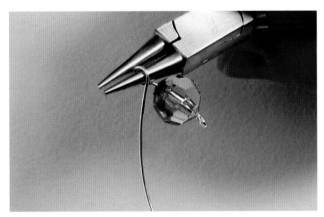

1 Thread the bead you have selected to wrap onto a spool of 20-gauge (0.8mm) wire.

2 Form a small loop at one end of the wire with your round-nosed pliers.

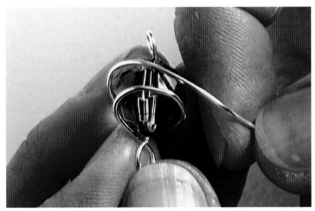

3 Twist the wire to form another loop at the other end of the bead and cut the wire off the spool, leaving about 6in. (15cm) of wire extending.

4 Wrap this wire around the bead in any fashion and as tightly as possible, using your fingers. Secure it around the top and bottom as well.

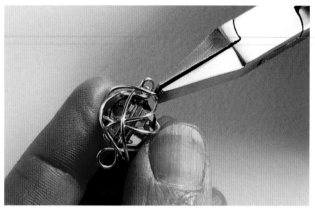

5 Secure the very end of the wire by wrapping it around one of the top loops, using your flat-nosed pliers.

6 Using just the very tips of your flat-nosed pliers, carefully twist or tweak the wires to tighten them around the encased bead.

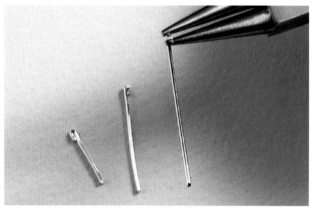

7 For the tassel, cut three varying lengths of wire and fold the ends into small headpins (see page 17). The lengths depend on how long you want the tassel to be.

8 Thread these wires with small beads and curl the other ends into links, using your round-nosed pliers.

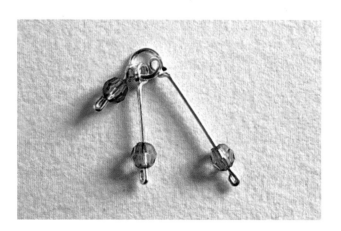

9 Place the three beaded rods on a jumpring (see page 20) and suspend this tassel from the bottom of your wrapped bead.

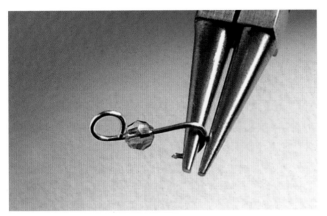

10 To create suspension link between the tassel and the chain, make an "S" link with a threaded bead. Cut a 1in. (2.5cm) length of wire. Make a loop at one end, thread on a bead, then make a loop in the opposite direction at the other end.

11 Connect the tasseled bead to the beaded "S" link, then add a jumpring to the top of the "S" link.

12 Wrap two smaller beads in the same way (steps 1 to 6) and link them to the jumpring. Add the chain to the other ends of the small beads. If you wish, you can break the chain by interspersing it with beads. Add your choice of fastener (see pages 22—26).

Wrapped Bead Earrings

To create the matching earrings, follow steps 1 to 6 of the necklace. Finish by making one tassel for suspension and attach to earwires. However, for something a little more elaborate, the full tassel can look very decorative.

Valentine's Jewelry

St. Valentine's day, on which birds were believed to mate and sweethearts were chosen, has become a traditional time to give a gift or card to a loved one. Giving heart-shaped items symbolizing love and romance has become a Western tradition and it is particularly satisfying to create something yourself to make the gift more personal. The decorative heart design shown here can be made into a necklace, earrings, or a keyring, or linked together to form a bracelet.

This delicate heart design created using wire and beads can be made into stunning jewelry, or even fixed to the front of a special hand-made Valentine card.

Valentine Heart Necklace

Some people sport crosses on chains, St. Christopher medallions, or their astrology signs, but this heart necklace symbolizes tenderness and compassion—perfect for the turbulent world we live in. And once you have made this, why not create matching earrings and a bracelet to complete the set?

YOU WILL NEED

20-gauge (0.8mm) silver-plated wire

16-gauge (0.6mm) silver-plated wire

Small glass beads, plus 1 seedbead

Wirecutters

Round-nosed pliers

Flat-nosed pliers

Hammer and steel block (optional)

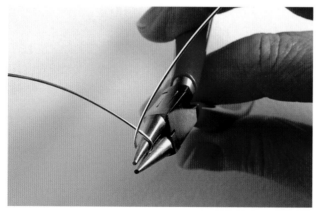

1 To create the centerpiece heart, cut a 5—6in. (12.5—15cm) length of 20-gauge (0.8mm) wire. (The length of wire required depends on how large or small you wish to make the piece.) Place your round-nosed pliers just past the center of the wire and form a loop by crossing one wire over in one direction and the other the opposite way, using round-nosed pliers.

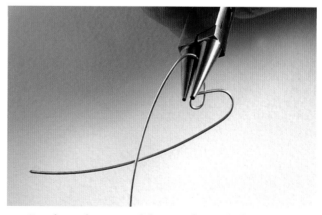

2 Put the widest part of the round-nosed pliers on either side of this central loop and pull each extended wire down to meet the other, forming a heart shape. (For a larger heart you can use a pen or wooden cylindrical dowel for shaping the rounded tops of the heart shape.)

3 Using the very ends of your round-nosed pliers, curl the wire outward into small circles on each side.

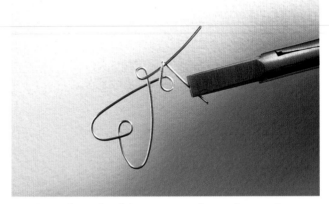

4 Bring the ends of the wire together and secure by wrapping the shorter end around the longer end.

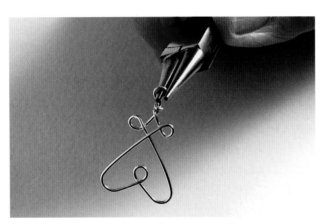

5 Cut off any excess wire, leaving about ⅓in. (1cm) to form a link, curling the end into a loop around your round-nosed pliers. If you wish, you can gently tap the shape with a hammer on a steel block to flatten and work-harden, being careful not to hammer any cross-over wires as this would weaken the metal.

6 Thread your central feature bead onto wire and form a small spiral at one end and a link at the other. Using flat-nosed pliers, connect this to the base link of your heart frame.

7 Using the thinner wire and working from the spool, thread a small seedbead and form a tiny spiral or head-pin at the bottom. Cut the wire about ⅓in. (1cm) above the bead. Form a link and attach to the center of the heart.

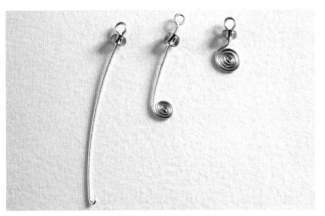

8 Cut a 2in. (5cm) length of the thicker wire. Using flat-nosed pliers, form a link at one end. Thread on a bead and make a spiral at the other end.

9 Repeat step 8 to make two beads and spirals to hang from the loops on each side of the heart.

10 The heart centerpiece can be suspended from a chain or cord of your choice. Alternatively, create an "S" link chain (see page 21), incorporating the same color beads to create an ornate and unified piece of jewelry.

Heart Earrings

To complete the set, these matching earrings are made in the same way as the necklace pendant and are suspended from silver earwires.

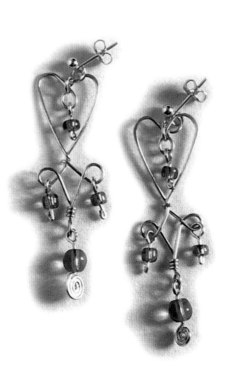

Heart Bracelet

This delicate bracelet, designed to match the necklace and earrings featured on the previous pages, is made by linking approximately seven small wire hearts together (the number of heart units used will depend on the diameter of your wrist). If you wish, you can connect threaded beads between the wire hearts to add a little variety to the chain—small, pastel-colored seedbeads are ideal for this.

YOU WILL NEED

20-gauge (0.8mm) wire

Beads

Hammer and steel block

Round-nosed pliers

Flat-nosed pliers

Wirecutters

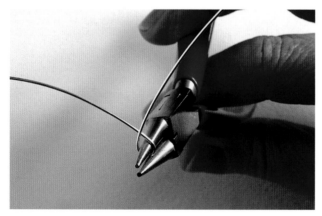

1 To create the heart shapes, cut 3½—4in. (9—10cm) of wire (or more for a larger heart shape). Find the approximate center and curl the wire around the end of your round-nosed pliers, crossing over each wire so that they face in opposite directions. Make six of these.

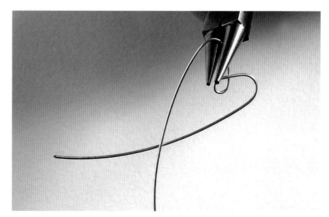

2 Place the widest part of your round-nosed pliers on each side of the central loop and pull the wires down on either side to form a heart shape (for a larger heart shape, use a wooden cylindrical dowel to form the rounded tops of the heart). Repeat for the other heart shapes.

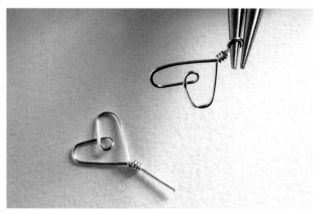

3 Using your round-nosed pliers, wrap the projecting wire around the stem of the heart. Form a link with this wire. This will become the point where all the units link together. Repeat for the other heart shapes.

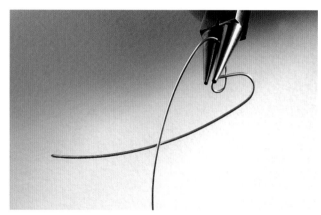

4 For the suspended heart pendant for the end of your bracelet, cut a 5in. (12.5cm) length of wire and, using round-nosed pliers, fold the wire around, leaving one side longer than the other. Wrap and secure one wire around the stem, as in step 2, but for this heart leave a longer stem.

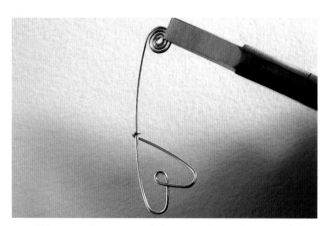

5 When you have created this extra heart shape, curl the end of the stem into a small decorative spiral, using flat-nosed pliers.

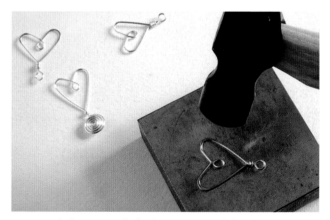

6 Gently hammer all the hearts to work-harden them. Take care not to hammer the wires where they cross over as this would weaken them.

7 Make eight jumprings, either by wrapping the wire around the widest part of your round-nosed pliers or around a cylindrical dowel (see page 20).

8 Make seven beaded "S" links. Cut 1in. (2.5cm) pieces of wire. Thread a bead into the center of each wire (see threaded beads, page 17), fold the wire at right angles using round-nosed pliers, and bring the wire back on itself to form a round link. Repeat at the other end.

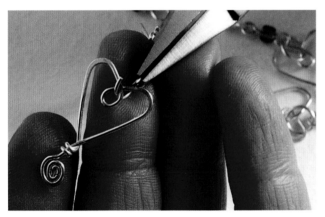

9 Join the bracelet together, connecting jumprings to the tops of the hearts, then the threaded beads. The suspended spiraled heart links at one end of the bracelet.

10 Make a fish hook fastener (see page 22) and attach to the other end of the bracelet.

Heart Keyring

When words just aren't enough, this beautiful heart-shaped keyring threaded with tiny glass beads makes the perfect gift for someone you love. And while you have all your wire, beads, and equipment to hand, assemble another one for yourself … because you're worth it!

YOU WILL NEED

20-gauge (0.8mm) silver-plated wire

16-gauge (0.6mm) silver-plated wire (optional)

Small glass beads

Ready-made keyring

Wirecutters

Round-nosed pliers

1 To create the heart shape, cut approximately 6in. (15cm) of wire (or more for a larger heart shape). Find the approximate center of this length and curl the wire around the end of your round-nosed pliers, crossing over each wire so that they face in opposite directions.

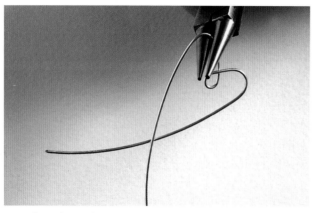

2 Place the widest part of your round-nosed pliers on each side of the central loop and pull the wires down on either side to form a heart shape (for a larger heart shape, you can use a wooden cylindrical dowel to form the rounded tops of the heart).

3 Thread the small beads onto the outer frame of the heart, either in a regular pattern or choosing different colors at random.

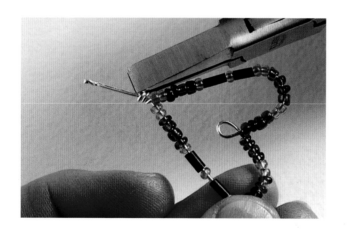

4 When the beads have been threaded all around the heart outline, bring the two ends of the wire together and, using flat-nosed pliers, wrap one wire neatly around the other to secure the beads in place, leaving enough wire projecting to make a link.

5 Thread larger beads onto the "stem" end wire and curl the surplus into a spiral, using round-nosed pliers, to provide an ornamental finish.

6 If desired, using the thinner wire, attach a small threaded bead (with a link at one end and a headpin at the other; see pages 21 and 17) and suspend from the inner central loop of the heart.

7 Connect a ready-made keyring to the central loop of your beaded heart using flat-nosed pliers (the keyring will probably have a jumpring already fitted to it). If the beaded heart becomes misshapen over time, simply bend it carefully back into shape.

Wedding Celebrations

Every bride wants to shine on her wedding day. Making your own jewelry for this occasion is both fun and rewarding, and allows you to personalize your wedding with beautiful accessories that make you look extra-special. Wedding jewelry makes a stylish statement on the big day and can be kept as a precious memento for years to come. When deciding on the design for your wedding jewelry, consider the style of your outfit. If the dress is very decorative with embroidery and embellishments, keep the jewelry unfussy; but for a simpler outfit, try something more dynamic and ornate.

Designing and making your own jewelry for your wedding day means you will have something extra-special that you can keep and wear on other celebratory occasions.

Edwardian Necklace

This design of this elegant Edwardian-style necklace takes its inspiration from the early twentieth century. It uses a ready-made chain and would be the ideal embellishment for any style of wedding dress with a low neckline. If you wish, for a special finishing touch, make your own chain (see pages 30—41). You could also substitute the pearls for crystal beads and the gold wire for silver to suit the fabrics or colors of your outfit.

YOU WILL NEED

Ready-made chain—enough to fit around your neck and for 24-gauge (0.6mm) wire to thread through the links

20-gauge (0.8mm) gold-plated wire

5 tiny pearl beads

2 larger pearl beads

Wirecutters

Round-nosed pliers

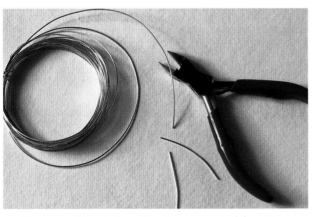

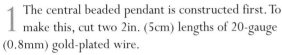

1 The central beaded pendant is constructed first. To
make this, cut two 2in. (5cm) lengths of 20-gauge
(0.8mm) gold-plated wire.

2 Using the round-nosed
pliers, find the center
of each wire and cross one
side over the other to create
a central loop.

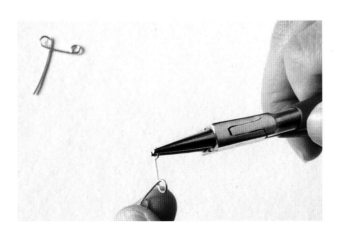

3 Curl the extended ends outward into small loops using
the ends of the round-nosed pliers. These will make up
the two halves of the pendant.

4 Create jumprings to link the pendant together by wrapping 20-gauge (0.8mm) wire around the round-nosed pliers to form a spring (see page 20). Cut each ring of the spring to create the links (see inset).

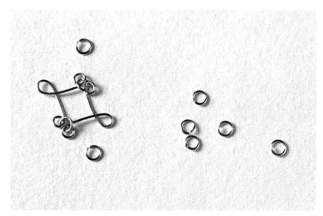

5 Connect the two halves of the pendant together on each side using the jumprings you have just made.

6 Thread the bead for the center of the pendant onto 20-gauge (0.8mm) wire, leaving ½in. (1cm) of wire on either side. Fold each wire end into a right angle, then back to form a loop. Do this on both sides and attach the loops to the top and bottom of the pendant.

7 To make the hanging beads on either side of the pendant, thread two smaller beads onto 20-gauge (0.8mm) wire, leaving ½in. (1cm) of wire on one side, and a little less on the other to form a headpin (see page 17). Attach these in the same way as in step 6.

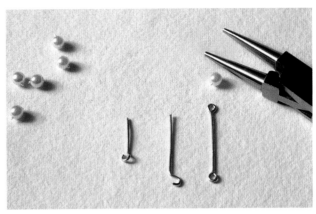

8 For the drop bead, thread a larger pearl onto 20-gauge (0.8mm) wire, forming links at both ends with your round-nosed pliers, as you did in step 6. Connect this to the bottom loop of the pendant.

9 To make the tassel, cut three lengths of 20-gauge (0.8mm) wire, graduating from about 1½in. (4cm) down. Form small loops at the ends of each length using the very end of the round-nosed pliers.

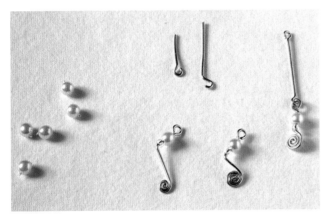

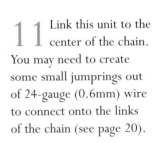

10 Thread three small beads onto 20-gauge (0.8mm) wire, leaving ½in. (1cm) at one end to form a link and at least 1½in. (4cm) at the other end to curl into a spiral. Connect all three spiraled pearls onto the tassel sticks to form the center of your necklace.

11 Link this unit to the center of the chain. You may need to create some small jumprings out of 24-gauge (0.6mm) wire to connect onto the links of the chain (see page 20).

Variations

For a more ornate effect, the chain can be interspersed at regular intervals by small pearls threaded onto 24-gauge (0.6mm) wire. For a necklace to suit a dress with a higher neckline, omit the tassel (steps 9 and 10).

Beaded Chain Variation

If you would like to make this Edwardian-style necklace more decorative (perhaps if your wedding dress has a classic, simple design), you can create a more elaborate chain by using "S" links interspersed at regular intervals with threaded beads. See pages 17 and 21 for the techniques.

Edwardian Earrings

To create drop earrings to match this necklace, simply follow steps 1—10 of the necklace and suspend the tops of the hangers from gold earwires.

Elizabethan Choker Necklace

This crystal and pearl necklace, inspired by sixteenth-century designs, would suit a high-necked dress. It could also be worn as a decorative headband.

YOU WILL NEED

Ready-made chain

Clear crystal and pearl beads, ⅛—¼in. (4—5mm) in diameter

20-gauge (0.8mm) gold-plated wire

Wirecutters

Round-nosed pliers

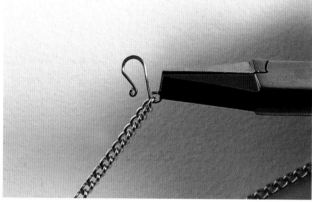

Variation

You can create a more ornate necklace and bracelet by making your own chain. Here we have used an "S" link chain (see page 21). If you wish, you can add extra crystals and pearls for a more elaborate design.

1 Measure and cut the amount of chain needed for the diameter of your neck, about 14—15in. (35—38cm). Don't forget that the fastener will add another 1in. (2.5cm) to the necklace. Create a fastener or clasp with 20-gauge (0.8mm) wire (see pages 22—26) and secure this to the ends of the chain.

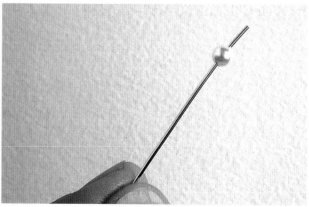

2 Cut nine 2in. (5cm) lengths of wire. Thread your crystal and pearl beads onto these wires.

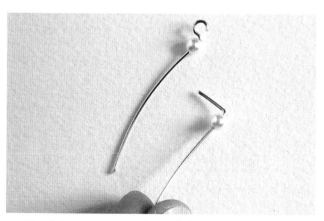

3 Bend the wires at a right angle ⅜in. (1cm) from the ends to form the link.

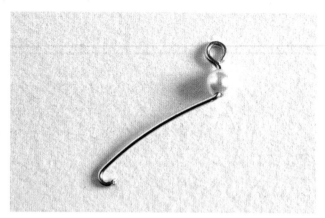

4 Using flat-nosed pliers, create a small hook at the other end of the wire.

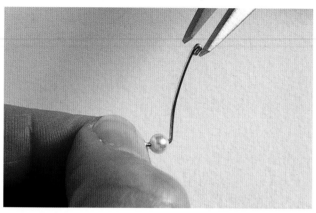

5 Squash the hook with round-nosed pliers to form a headpin (see page 17).

6 Create a spiral at the other end with flat-nosed pliers (see page 18). Create nine of these, in a mix of crystals and pearls, to suspend from the front of the necklace.

7 Link these spiraled beads directly onto the chain, spacing at regular intervals with 4—6 links inbetween. It is easiest to start at the center of the necklace and work out on either side to achieve symmetry in your piece. Alternate the crystals and pearls.

Elizabethan Bracelet

The matching bracelet is created in exactly the same way as the choker necklace, but obviously needs less chain. For a standard wrist you will need about 6in. (15cm) of ready-made chain, allowing another 1in. (2.5cm) for the clasp. You might also decide to use smaller, more delicate crystal and pearl beads.

Elizabethan Earrings

Use the same tiny crystal and pearl beads as featured in the Elizabethan-style choker necklace on page 92 to create a matching pair of shimmering earrings.

1 Thread two crystal and two pearl beads onto 20-gauge (0.8mm) wire for each earring (as in step 3 of the necklace), creating a link at one end and a spiral at the other. Link one crystal and one pearl threaded bead onto a jumpring (see page 20). Repeat this process so that you end up with two pairs of linked beads for each earring.

2 Cut a short piece of ready-made chain (about four links long) and connect the jumpring (threaded with a pair of crystal and pearl beads) at each end.

3 Thread a ready-made earwire through the top link of the chain to create a bunched effect. Connect the second bunch. If you wish, you could add more beads for a fuller look.

Wedding Wands

For young bridesmaids or flower-girls, these elegant ribboned wands are perfect supplements to bouquets of flowers. A bunch of wands in different designs could even be carried on their own as a unique "posy." After the wedding, the wands can be kept as charming mementos of the special day. If you prefer, instead of using white silk ribbons, choose a color to match the bridesmaids' dresses or bouquets.

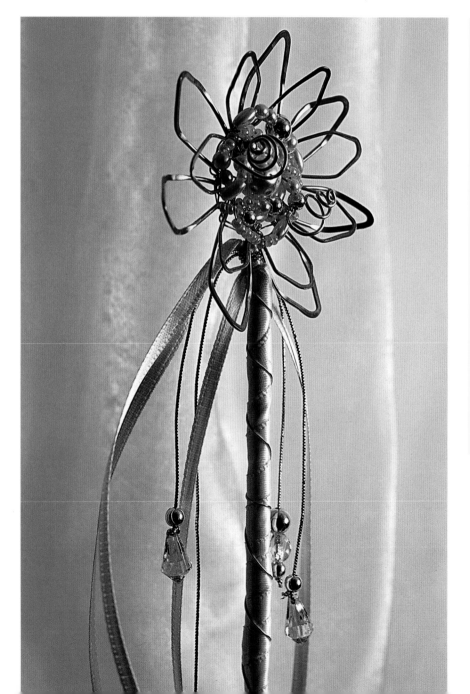

YOU WILL NEED

20-gauge (0.8mm) gold-plated wire

28-gauge (0.4mm) gold-plated wire

Assortment of pearl, crystal, and gold beads

1 wooden flower stick

White silk ribbon and colored thin ribbons for decoration

Wirecutters

Round-nosed pliers

Flat-nosed pliers

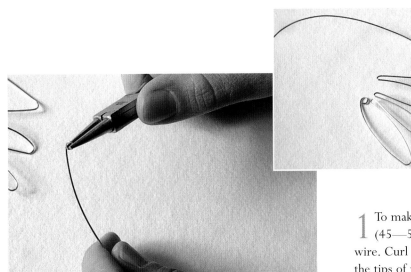

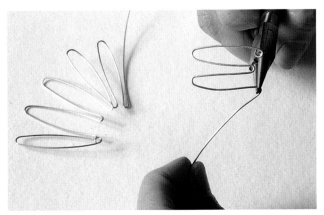

1 To make the flower petals, cut two 18—20 in. (45—50cm) lengths of 20-gauge (0.8mm) gold-plated wire. Curl one end of each length into a small loop with the tips of your round-nosed pliers.

2 Using the round-nosed pliers, bend both lengths into a zig-zag pattern. The height of each zig-zag should be approximately 1—1⅛in. (2.5—4cm).

3 When all the wire has been used, bring both ends together, forming a circular shape, and thread one end through the first loop to secure. You should now have two rough flower shapes that are approximately the same size.

4 To create more shapely petals, squeeze the very ends of each petal with the flat-nosed pliers and then open the centers by placing the pliers inside each petal shape. Spend a little time forming the wire flower frames into pleasing shapes.

5 Take both wire flower frames and place one on top of the other. Bind and secure these together, by weaving 28-gauge (0.4mm) wire around the centers.

6 Thread the remaining wire with an assortment of pearl, crystal, and gold-colored beads, weaving and securing them into the center of your flower.

7 Continue weaving and attaching the beads in this way until you are satisfied with the appearance of the flower. The center of the flower should look full, with the different types of beads evenly distributed.

8 Using fine wire, secure the flower onto the flower stick from the back. Wrap silk ribbons around the stem of the stick and fasten this with 28-gauge (0.4mm) wire spiraling down the stem. Thread some beads onto thin ribbons and tie them to the top of the wand.

Variations

The wire flower or heart shapes that form the top of the wands can also be used to make attractive hair ornaments, brooches, or hat decorations. Simply follow steps 1 to 7 of the project and let your imagination inspire you. Attach ready-made hair combs, brooch fasteners, or hat pins to complete the pieces.

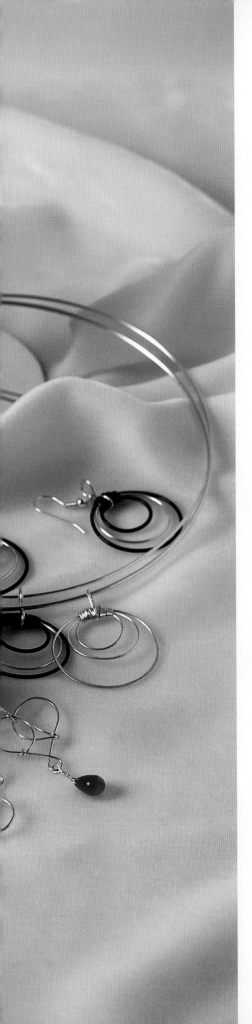

Classic
Collections

It is always very rewarding to create a stylish set of jewelry, either to wear on a special occasion, or as a unique and memorable gift for a friend or member of the family. The Classic Collections featured in this chapter are perfect to make and give as special presents. Once you have some experience and confidence in creating your own wire jewelry, you can choose to follow the basic principles of each project loosely, adding your own individual flair. When you are confident in your skills, substitute your plated wire for sterling silver or precious gold, and your glass beads for semi-precious stones.

There are four distinctly different styles of jewelry featured in this chapter, all inspired by classic designs—Art Deco, Greek, Egyptian, and Sixties style.

Egyptian Classic Set

The technique used in this Egyptian-style project is a quick yet very effective way of creating wire jewelry with the appearance of chain mail. You could also experiment with making different combinations of looped rows, to design either rectangular or square pieces. On pages 106 to 107, the verdigris paint technique shows how to add an aged effect to the jewelry.

YOU WILL NEED:

20-gauge (0.8mm) wire

Bead of your choice

Round-nosed pliers

Flat-nosed pliers

Hammer and steel block

Wirecutters

1 Working from a coil of 20-gauge (0.8mm) wire, form a small loop at one end by curling it around the tips of your round-nosed pliers.

2 Reposition your pliers beside the first loop and form another loop. The top wire should twist over the lower wire in the same direction as the first loop.

3 Continue shaping the wire into loops around the jaws of the pliers, until you have formed a row of seven complete circular loops.

4 Using wirecutters, snip off the loops from the coil, giving you a row of loops.

5 Repeat steps 1 to 4 to create another wire row with six circles, then make rows with five, four, three, and finally two circles.

6 Very gently flatten the pieces, by tapping them with a hammer. Be careful not to hammer where the wires cross as this will weaken the wire.

7 Make approximately 16 jumprings (see page 20). Connect all looped rows together at their ends in descending order, using 14 of the jumprings.

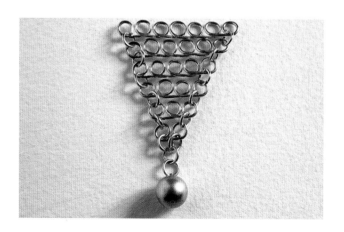

8 Join the drop bead to the base of the looped triangle, using the two remaining jumprings and the flat-nosed pliers. As well as looking decorative, the weight of this bead will help the triangle to hang properly, so the rows of jumprings are perfectly displayed.

9 Create an "S" link chain from 20-gauge (0.8mm) wire (see page 21) and join to the outer loops on the top row of the looped triangle.

10 Make an "S" link fastener from matching wire (see page 24) and attach it to the end of the chain to complete the design.

Egyptian Earrings

These matching earrings are constructed in exactly the same way as the necklace, except that they are suspended the other way round, with the apex of the triangle at the top, attached to earwires, and embellished with drop beads hanging from the bottom row.

Egyptian "Verdigris"

Any of the projects contained in this book can look completely different by varying bead sizes, colors, and wire gauges. It is possible to purchase wires in every color of the rainbow, but alternatively, as in this Egyptian design, you can color the wire yourself. Spray paint (sold for use on cars) and enamel craft paints are available from do-it-yourself stores or hobby stores.

The verdigris Egyptian necklace design was constructed out of 20-gauge (0.8mm) copper wire with a chain created from "S" links threaded with small turquoise seedbeads. A small spiral of wire is suspended from the end of the necklace for decoration.

The earrings are also created out of 20-gauge (0.8mm) copper wire, with decorative ends made from turquoise seedbeads threaded onto spiraled wire. The tops of the earrings are created by making two closed spirals with ready-made ear-posts glued to the backs. (For non-pierced ears, clips can be substituted.)

TIP

Place the piece you wish to verdigris on an old piece of newspaper within a box. Ensure that your room is well ventilated as the spray varnish has a very pungent smell (you could do this outside in fine weather).

YOU WILL NEED

Pale green paint

A hard, stippling brush

Clear matte varnish spray

Kitchen paper

1 Pour a little paint out into a container and dab the end of your paint brush in it. Stipple this paint onto your piece of jewelry, coating the entire surface.

2 Where the painted areas look too heavy, gently dab the paint off with a piece of kitchen paper. Keep adding the paint and dabbing it off until you are happy with the overall effect.

3 When the jewelry is dry and coated on both sides, finish by spraying the entire surface with a clear, matte varnish to fix the paint and prevent it from flaking off through wear and tear. Leave to dry.

Greek Geometric Bracelet

If you've never made a square unit like this classic Greek key symbol before, practice on a length of spare wire before using your good silver wire. It usually takes a couple of attempts to create even geometric pieces, but once you've mastered the technique, this bracelet is an easy jewelry design to make.

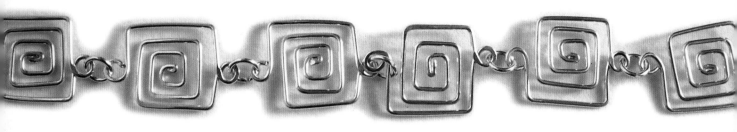

YOU WILL NEED

20-gauge (0.8 mm) wire

Wirecutters

Round-nosed pliers

Flat-nosed or snipe-nosed pliers

Hammer and steel block

1 Depending on the size of each geometric unit, cut approximately seven 4½—5in. (11.5—12.5cm) lengths of 20-gauge (0.8mm) wire.

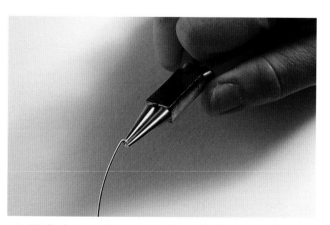

2 With the tips of your round-nosed pliers, curl the ends of these wires into tiny hooks and squeeze these flat on themselves (as you would to make a headpin, see page 17).

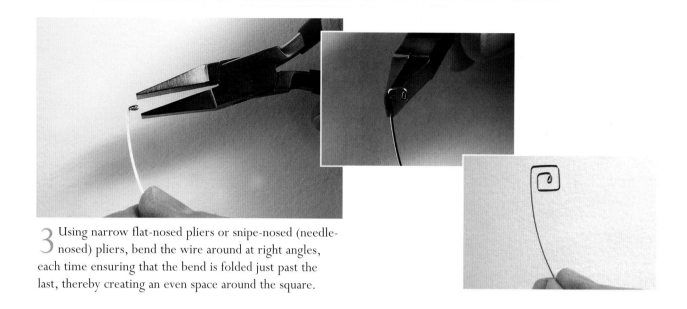

3 Using narrow flat-nosed pliers or snipe-nosed (needle-nosed) pliers, bend the wire around at right angles, each time ensuring that the bend is folded just past the last, thereby creating an even space around the square.

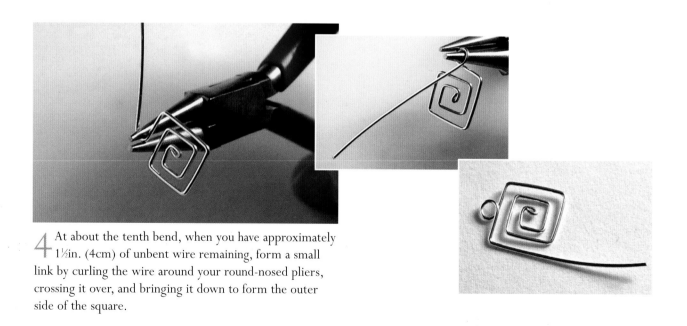

4 At about the tenth bend, when you have approximately 1½in. (4cm) of unbent wire remaining, form a small link by curling the wire around your round-nosed pliers, crossing it over, and bringing it down to form the outer side of the square.

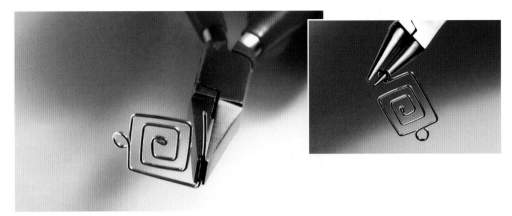

5 Create another link at the end of the wire in the same
way, parallel with the cross-over link on the other side
of the square.

6 Flatten and gently tap each unit with your hammer (be
careful not to hammer the cross-over link or you will
weaken the wire).

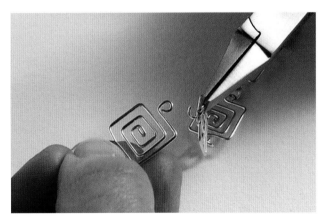

7 Attach all units together with jumprings (see page 20)
and create a fastener for the bracelet in matching wire
(see pages 22—26).

Greek Geometric Earrings

These earrings are created in the same way as the bracelet units, by following steps 1 to 6. The small suspended squares are created similarly, however, instead of step 4 (where the wire is crossed over) just bend the wire up at a right angle, thread on a bead, and form a loop at the top to suspend the bead from your geometric unit. To complete the earrings, connect both pieces onto earwires.

1 Follow steps 1 to 6 of the Greek Geometric Bracelet, creating two geometric units.

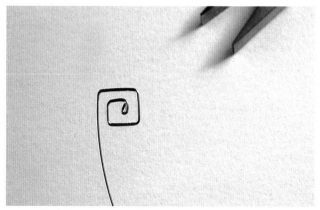

2 Fold the wire as before, using flat-nosed pliers, creating the square geometric shape.

3 Create a smaller geometric wire square following steps 1 to 4 of the bracelet, and instead of making a link, thread a bead onto the projecting wire and then secure with a link.

4 Connect this beaded unit to the geometric square and suspend from an earwire.

Variation

The Ancient Greeks used beads painted with the symbol of an eye to ward off evil spirits and to protect themselves from harm. For an authentic touch, include "eye" beads in your jewelry.

Art Deco Necklace

The Art Deco necklace has such an elegant design, with its gently curving loops and hanging bead. You can easily improvise on this design by hanging it upside down or by reducing or enlarging the design.

YOU WILL NEED

20-gauge (0.8mm) wire
Beads
Ready-made chain
Wirecutters
Round-nosed pliers
Cylindrical dowel
Hammer and steel block

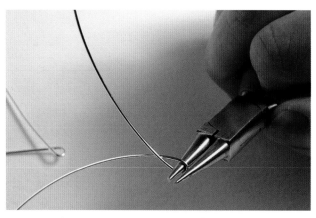

1 Begin by cutting two 6in. (15cm) lengths of 20-gauge (0.8mm) wire. Find the center of each wire with your round-nosed pliers and cross the wires over.

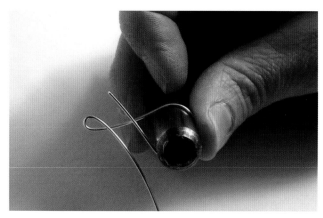

2 Using a cylindrical dowel (the shaft of a thick pen will do) curl the wires, loosely around the cylindrical form to create two large loops facing away from each other (and the center) until they cross over the outer frame.

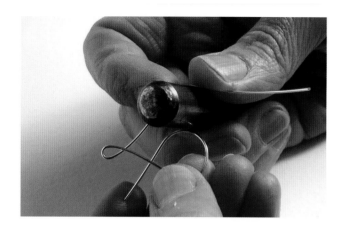

3 Using the dowel, form a similar circular loop on the other side of the frame, as in step 2.

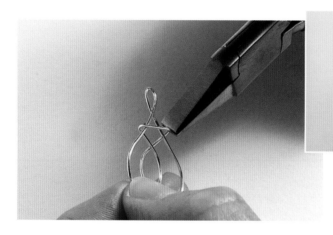

4 Secure the projecting ends of the wire around the main framework of the piece by wrapping it near the top central link.

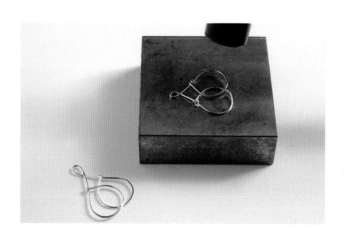

5 Gently hammer the pieces on a steel block to straighten and flatten them. Be careful not to hammer on any crossed over wires as this will weaken them.

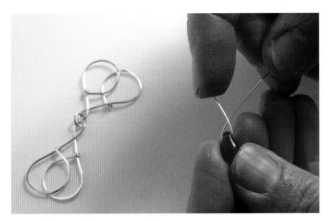

6 When you have created two identical units, connect them together with jumprings (see page 20), using your flat-nosed pliers.

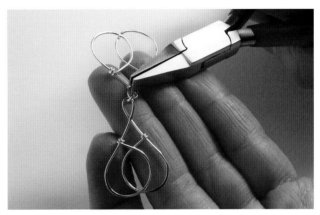

7 Thread a small bead with wire to form the center of your necklace.

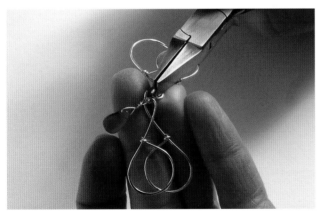

8 Connect this bead to the center of the units, using flat-nosed pliers. Ensure that the link is securely closed.

9 To make the chain, thread your chosen beads onto wires (see page 17).

10 Using round-nosed plires, form links on each side of your threaded beads.

11 Using wirecutters, cut the ready-made chain in short, equal lengths.

12 Link the threaded beads onto the chain at regular intervals, using flat-nosed pliers.

13 Link the chain to your central unit, making sure the sides are symmetrical. Add a clasp of your choice, made from the same wire as the rest of the necklace (see pages 22—26).

Art Deco Earrings

These earrings should be made slightly smaller than the necklace centerpiece by using 5in. (12.5cm) lengths of 20-gauge (0.8mm) wire. Follow steps 1 to 5 of the necklace, then continue as shown below.

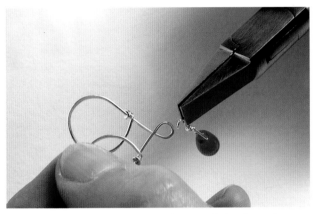

1 Thread a bead onto wire and suspend this from the looped end of the unit.

2 Connect earwires to the other end. Repeat to make the second earring.

Art Nouveau

This variation is created in a similar way to the Art Deco design, but is more elaborate. The chain is made with threaded beads, interspersed with beaded "S" links. The centerpiece has a tasseled pendant, and the earrings have been suspended in the opposite direction to the Art Deco earrings, shown above.

Sixties Hoop Set

There are endless variations to this classic modern design. Beads can

be threaded onto the hoops for extra color and ornamentation, or alternatively,

you can create the hoops in wires of different colors.

YOU WILL NEED

20-gauge (0.8mm) wire (or 18-gauge (1mm) wire for a chunkier look)

3 cylindrical dowels of varying diameters to shape your hoops

Masking tape

28-gauge (0.4mm) fine binding wire

Ready-made choker wire

Wirecutters

Round-nosed pliers

Flat-nosed pliers

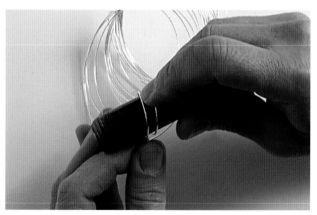

1 Begin by wrapping 20-gauge (0.8mm) wire around the three cylindrical dowels to form wire hoops with different diameters.

2 When the hoops are cut, the circles will spring open. Spend a little time closing and forming the wire into even circles.

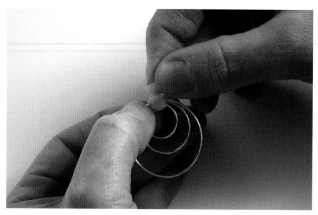

3 Position the three hoops within each other and tape together at the top with masking tape to secure and to hide the join of the circles.

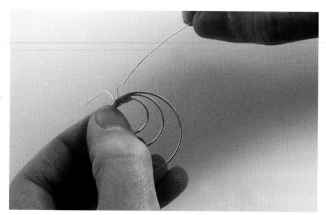

4 Cut a generous length of 28-gauge (0.4mm) fine binding wire and wrap this tightly over the masking tape join to conceal it.

5 Using wirecutters, cut the end of the fine binding wire close to the hoops, ensuring that the cut end does not protrude outward.

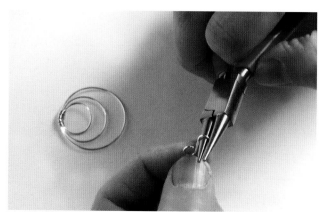

6 To created the suspension hook, snip a 1in. (2.5cm) length of 20-gauge (0.8mm) wire and form an "S" link (see page 21).

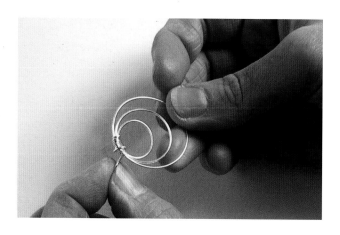

7 Carefully open up one end of the "S" link and thread this through the middle of the three bound hoops, close to the binding.

 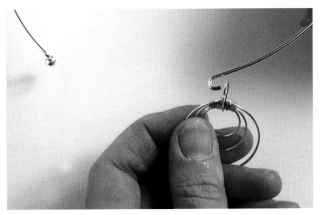

8 Using your flat-nosed pliers, squeeze the end of the "S" link around the top to secure.

9 Hang the pendant from the ready-made choker wire by theading it through the "S" link.

Sixties Hoop Earrings

The matching three-hooped earrings are made by following steps 1 to 8 of the necklace. Finish by connecting them to ready-made silver earwires. As a variation, you could use contrasting colors of wire for the different sizes of hoops.

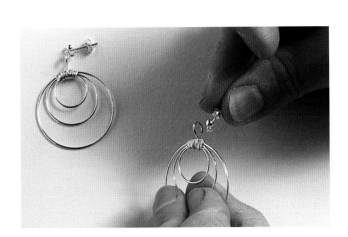 

Glossary

Chain-nosed pliers
See snipe-nosed pliers.

Dowel
A cylindrical object to curve wire around. You could use a wooden dowel, a knitting needle, a rolling pin, the handle of a wooden spoon, or anything cylindrical to hand.

Earwires
Ready-made earring fittings which can be bought from jewelry suppliers.

Findings
A term used for jewelry components, such as brooch bars, chains, keyrings, earring posts, leather cord, etc.

Flat-nosed pliers
Smooth-jawed, parallel pliers which provide a vice-like grip for holding wire.

Gauge
Refers to the thickness of wire. The smaller the number, the thicker the gauge; for example, 14-gauge (1.5mm) wire, 18-gauge (1mm) wire, 20-gauge (0.8mm) wire, 24-gauge (0.6mm) wire and 28-gauge (0.4mm) wire.

Headpin
A piece of wire which has been folded at the end into a knob, so that a threaded bead can be suspended without slipping off. You can buy ready-made headpins from suppliers or make your own (see page 17).

Jumprings
The most elemental link you can create. They can serve as many individual units to form a chain, or used individually to join (or jump) a series of units together, as in a beaded necklace or bracelet.

Link or Loop
A full circle of wire, used for connecting or linking purposes.

Mandrel
A circular shape, usually made from wood or steel, for curving metal.

Round-nosed pliers
Tapered cone pliers, used for curling and forming links and loops in wire.

Shank
The part of a ring that encircles the finger.

Snipe-nosed pliers
Sometimes referred to as needle-nosed pliers or chain-nosed pliers. Smooth-jawed, parallel pliers with tapered ends which are used for delicate jewelry-making work.

Snips
See wirecutters.

Spool
A coil of wire that can be obtained in measured reels from craft stores and hobby suppliers.

Steel block
A perfectly flat block of steel, used with a flat-ended hammer to work-harden and flatten metal.

Temper
To toughen or work harden wire by hammering, coiling, twisting, and forming it, reducing its workability.

Wirecutters
Sometimes referred to as snips. For wire work these should be small with jaws that end in a point, allowing you to cut into the wire from any angle.

Work-harden
Refers to the fact that the more you move and manipulate metal wire, the harder and less flexible it becomes. Gentle hammering helps to work-harden wire, so that it becomes tough enough to be made into wearable jewelry that should not fall apart.

Suppliers

As well as buying from your local craft or hobby stores, try browsing these websites to see the wide range of wires and beads that you can order.

UK Websites

www.beadaddict.co.uk

www.beadsunlimited.co.uk

www.beadworks.co.uk

www.constellationbeads.co.uk

www.creativebeadcraft.co.uk

www.gjbeads.co.uk

www.internationalcraft.com

www.jillybeads.com

www.rockingrabbit.co.uk

www.spangles4beads.co.uk

www.spellboundbead.co.uk

www.thebeadexclusive.com

www.wirejewellery.co.uk

US Websites

www.ballybead.com

www.beadalon.com

www.beadsandpieces.com

www.firemountaingems.com

www.gems2behold.com

www.jewelrysupply.com

www.landofodds.com

www.rings-things.com

www.vitabeads.com

www.wigjig.com

Index

Acknowledgments

Grateful thanks to the people who helped toward the publication of this book. First and foremost to Cindy Richards who gave me this opportunity; also to Georgina Harris, to Jacqui Hurst for her patience and skill in photography, and to Gillian Haslam who made sense of everything I have written.

Finally, I would like to thank my parents, Marian and Hans, for their endless love, support, and encouragement.